Clara Mason Fox

Pioneer, Painter, and Poet
of Orange County, California

Nov. 10, 2013

Dear Russ,

It's always good to keep connections
with people from the past. I'm so
glad you kept in touch! I hope you
enjoy reading the book. I think
you'll like Chapter 5!

Love,
Louraine

Clara Mason Fox

Pioneer, Painter, and Poet
of Orange County, California

Lorraine Passero

MILL CITY PRESS, MINNEAPOLIS

Mill City Press, Inc.
212 3rd Avenue North, Suite 290
Minneapolis, MN 55401
612.455.2294
www.millcitypublishing.com

ISBN-13: 978-1-62652-008-0
LCCN: 2013901767

Book Design by Mary Kristin Ross
Back cover photo by Cynthia Tyler

Printed in the United States of America

For my family and William

CONTENTS

ACKNOWLEDGMENTS

I have a wonderful team of people to thank. Each one of them guided me and offered their enthusiastic support while writing this book. Rochelle Mancini and Janet Whitcomb are two talented women who checked the facts and carefully edited the manuscript. Orange County historian Phil Brigandi and Assistant Archivist Chris Jepsen from the Orange County Archives assisted me in navigating through extensive records to find what I needed. Across the country in New York City, Archives Librarian Carol Salomon provided me with historical documents from the Cooper Union Archives Department. Susan Carter gave me artistic direction in designing the book cover.

Clara Mason Fox's niece Gwen and her husband Boyd Johnson willingly took time to share stories of their Aunt Clara, through emails, phone calls, and during a visit to Colorado. Lucille Cruz is more than Silverado's librarian; she is the canyon's local historian who directed me to many of the sources used during the course of my research. Marian Norris from Heritage Hill Historical Park in Lake Forest was invaluable in tracking down information and pictures of old El Toro.

I am appreciative of my family and friends for their encouragement during the writing process. I especially want to thank my husband Jon, not only for his artistic ancestry, but also for cooking dinner on numerous occasions while I was busy typing and conducting online research. Lastly, I am grateful to Clara Mason Fox, and to her niece, Marge Seeman, for having the foresight to preserve artwork, family photos, and letters for future generations to discover and appreciate.

Chapter One

A Box in the Attic

No one had been in Grandma Marge's attic for years. I would find out that the corner cottage with small paned windows on Glenneyre Street in Laguna Beach, where Grandma Marge had spent so much of her life, seemed to hold a great many mysteries. Little did I know, when I first explored that attic, how many secrets I would come to learn over time—all because of a box hidden away in a corner and left unnoticed for decades.

What we *did* know was that my husband Jon's Grandma Marge had lived in the seaside bungalow since it was built in 1925, and that she had continued to stay there alone for many long years after her husband Ed Seeman passed away. But we *didn't* know what a treasure trove of family memories we would find until we had to clean out the house after Grandma Marge, too, passed away in 1984.

Have you ever held a seashell to your ear? If you are very quiet, the sound of the ocean can be heard inside of it. The house by the sea was now like a shell. Walking through the doorway in silence I imagined so many memories it held inside its walls. How many times we sat around the old round wooden kitchen table, feasting on Grandma's pot roast and gravy while sharing stories of the latest happenings. A fire crackling and spewing in the fireplace on winter days gave us warmth and comfort in the midst of chilling ocean winds. Grandma always sat nearby in a small rocking chair just right for her petite frame, adding bits of wood to keep the fire going. Summertime meant bright sunny days at the beach, just a short walk down the cliff. Exhausted and hungry from swimming, we would hurriedly rinse the sand from our feet with icy cold hose water next to the back door before entering Grandma's house though the kitchen. Something tasty, like a couple of oatmeal raisin cookies or thick slices of homemade bread and strawberry jam, could always be found on the kitchen counter.

Now the house had a different feeling: it was as lifeless and quiet as a classroom after the students have gone home on the last day of school. We were brought back to the reality of our visit. The house needed to be cleaned out. Starting with the first floor, we cleared away

Grandma Marge's attic window

the furnishings and removed dusty paintings of wildflowers and desert landscapes. Next, it was time to check what we would find upstairs in the attic. We climbed the worn, creaky, wooden staircase and entered a low-angled attic room where tattered curtains filtered light streaming through the window. Faded wallpaper with a tiny floral pattern covered the walls. I wondered how many years had gone by since anyone had made the climb to this room.

At first, we only saw the expected things to be found in a room used for storage: long-forgotten pieces of broken furniture, piles of tattered clothing, and stacks of books. But then an old carton sitting in the corner caught my eye. Put a curious person together with a mysterious old box and guess what happens! I quickly pried open the box, shaking loose a cloud of dust to find its contents. Lying neatly inside were several small sketchbooks with old-fashioned covers. Next to them was a collection of letters, handwritten in pen and ink that had faded from black to faint

Attic room

gray. In a packet carefully tied with string, I found pages of poetry, along with photographs that once had been shiny and new, but now were ghostlike.

While Jon and other family members were busy cleaning, I took a break and sat on the floor in the hobbit-sized attic room to take a closer look at what I had just found. Carefully, I leafed through the frail, cream-colored pages of the sketchbooks. Who had created these detailed pencil drawings of sunbathers dressed in long swimming outfits? Beach scenes crowded the surface of the paper, as if not to waste any available space on the page. I blew away another cloud of dust to uncover a mysterious scrawl on the cover of the sketchbook. The words said 'Arch Beach, August 1894' and bore a signature: Clara L. Mason.

Clara's signature

The more I sifted through the drawings and writings, the more inquisitive I became. Who was Clara Mason? Why were her drawings and poetry saved in the house for so many years? And what was it that made me certain that I needed to find the answers?

Family heirlooms reach across the years to connect us with the past. In my case, just before she died, Grandma Marge had given my husband Jon a wonderful little rocking chair with a green velvet seat. For years, I rocked our daughter Inaeko to sleep in that comfortable chair I loved so much. Imagine how I felt when I saw the sketch you see below. It was of Clara's own mother sitting in the very same chair.

(Top) 1896 sketch of Clara's mother in rocking completed in one hour. (Right) Our daughter Inaeko in the same rocker (1984).

Clara and I became connected in ways I couldn't easily explain. I began a search to find out more about her. Our first connection I discovered early on was that we both loved to draw. Both of us also had been school teachers. Then, reading through a pile of letters, I found out that Clara had journeyed all the way from California to New York City to study art at Cooper Union. *New York City!* What a long distance away that was for a young girl to travel back in those days. And New York is where I had grown up. I couldn't help identifying more and more with Clara.

Living in the late 1800s, the Victorian Era, women were expected to stay home, take care of the family, and do the household chores. But Clara had achieved much more than most women living during those times. I knew I must learn as much as possible about such a remarkable woman.

In time, other members of the family learned of my interest in Clara Mason. One relative had a copy of a book Clara had owned, Charles Dickens' *Great Expectations*, containing interesting inscriptions. Another mystery to solve!

I decided to take the sketchbooks to the Laguna Beach Art Museum. The curator at the museum told me that, prior to seeing Clara's sketches, the earliest artwork portraying the area dated from the early 1900s. Clara's drawings were dated 1894! The curator was excited enough about this discovery to display Clara's sketches in the museum.

Historical research is like playing with a jigsaw puzzle. You find one piece of the puzzle, and then you start noticing the design that you have completed. Then you wonder about the space that is left to one side of the piece you just found, so you go off on another quest.

Over time I gathered bits and pieces about Clara Mason's life. It had started, of course, with the puzzling pieces of information discovered in the attic. Then after talking to family members I learned she was my husband Jon's great-great aunt. Trips to the Orange County Archives, libraries, and Heritage Hill Historical Park—where there is so much to learn about Orange County's history—gave me census information and stories from the past. More details of Clara's life surfaced through sources on the Internet. As I looked into one part of her life, I found myself asking additional questions about another part of her story.

For example, while visiting Laguna Beach's City Hall to check into the history of Grandma Marge's house, I came across an interesting document. The document stated that the house was designed by her niece, Clara Mason, who had written the history of El Toro. That one sentence opened yet another path to follow. More new information—and questions—unfolded when I visited the library staffed by the Saddleback Area Historical Society. That was where I found photos of places depicted in Clara's sketchbooks. I learned that Clara Mason was considered a scholarly lady, held in such high esteem by the local women's club that its members had asked her to write a history of their town.

In addition to studying documents, I had the chance to find out about Clara's life by talking to people who had personally known her and recognized her talents as an artist and writer. Clara began to reveal herself to me in a very special way. It was as if she wanted me to tell her story. Often I felt as though she was guiding me to people and places providing additional answers about who she was.

I came to know Clara's insights, dating from more than 75 years ago, about nature, history, and what she valued in life. Looking again and again at her drawings and reading her El Toro history and poetry, I saw through her eyes what was important to her. These creative forms of expression from the nineteenth and early twentieth centuries can provide an understanding of people's thoughts and feelings, the way social networking gives us a way to communicate today.

So come along with me on the journey to get to know Clara Mason Fox—a determined and talented Orange County, California pioneer woman—as you read what I learned about her life.

Who knows? Maybe Clara's story will lead you to discover your own family treasure box hidden away in a dusty attic.

Chapter Two

The Making of a Pioneer Girl

Just eight years after the Civil War ended, Clara Mason was born in Jackson Township, Ohio, on November 24, 1873. Our country had been divided like a piece of paper creased across the middle, in a war when a man living in the North could fight against his brother living in the South. Northerners were opposed to slavery and wanted the United States to remain united as one country. The Southerners profited from slave labor and were willing to become a separate country to keep slavery legal.

Clara at one year old

Once the war ended in 1865, times became tough, especially for farmers. During the war more crops than usual were needed to feed soldiers. Farmers had borrowed money to buy farm equipment and supplies to meet the crop demand. When the war ended, however, so did the increased food demand. Farmers were left in debt. Clara's parents, Nancy and George Mason, were one of the farming families who struggled to pay the debts they owed.

The Masons were hard working, self-sufficient people, used to growing enough food to feed their family through difficult economic times. Their children soon learned about responsibility and the importance of caring for each other to survive. Clara was the youngest of the three children, the oldest being her brother Charley and sister Nellie.

As you can see from her picture, Clara was a sweet-looking girl. Her eyes were large and dark and her silky brown hair was twisted into a top curl. In the photo she looks much like any little girl you might see playing in a park today. Life back in the 1800s, however, was quite different. Today kids complain about chores such as loading the dishwasher or taking out the trash. Let's take a closer look at what life for Clara was like.

Clara at age four

Farms were a distance from one another, so families were isolated. Stores could be miles away and neighbors and doctors were not always close by. Being self-sufficient meant the family grew crops and raised or hunted animals for food. Any surplus, or extra food, was stored for winter or sold at market. The Masons also bartered by exchanging some of their surplus for items they needed.

Storms, harsh winds, rain, and sun were elements that impacted the family's food supply and survival. So farmers were in sync with the seasons. Spring was welcomed with its mild weather when budding plants popped through the thawing ground. Hot winds blowing across the field on warm, sunny days signaled it was summer. Or the weather could quickly change, with dark gray clouds bringing heavy summer rains. A good crop season would yield plenty of sweet corn, ripe melons, and crisp green beans.

Autumn meant it was time for the fattened pigs to be slaughtered. Meat was then salt cured or smoked to last through the winter months. The crack of gunshot rang through the golden fields as migrating wild turkeys and ducks provided another source of food in the fall.

Winter arrived in Ohio with a cold slap. Record breaking temperatures dropped as low as minus two degrees the year Clara was born. Freezing rain and ice glazed the dirt roads, wooden barns, and houses. Snow and high winds forced Clara and her siblings to stay indoors for days. Children were expected to entertain themselves by playing with handmade dolls or with a game of ball and jacks. Reading or drawing pictures by the light of a kerosene lantern were favorite pastimes as well.

Keeping busy might have distracted them from the possibility of a tornado touching down on their house. Today, we can analyze computer data to predict tornadoes. However, in the 1800s, a severe thunderstorm was the only warning sign of a possible tornado arising. Then as now, most tornadoes occurred in the late afternoon or early evening during the spring and summer months. Fierce winds caused trees to topple onto houses, forcing everyone to take shelter in cellars until the tornado passed.

Except in times of disaster, chores had to be done, whether it was raining, snowing, or hot. Clara was expected, at a very young age, to do her share of the farm work along with

Charley, who was nine years older, and Nellie who was older by three years. Chores were a necessary part of a day that began at 4 a.m. After eating breakfast, by candlelight during the dark mornings, the mooing cows expected to be milked, clucking chickens waited to be fed, and hard-working horses needed brushing. The snow-covered barn that housed the animals had to be cleaned, even in the frost of winter.

Washing clothes meant scrubbing them on a washboard in a big tub, then hanging them to dry on a clothesline. Time was taken to sew clothes, one careful stitch at a time, so they lasted for several years. A tear on a shirt or pants was mended with a pair of scissors, needle, and thread. Early on, young girls were judged by how neatly they could sew a seam or make a torn shirt look good as new. It was one of the necessary skills needed to become a good wife.

For breakfast, Clara and her family did not go to the nearest fast food drive-thru for a breakfast egg burrito. Instead, eggs were gathered from their barn each morning. Imagine the kitchen smells of sweet corn muffins or freshly baked bread. Hot pans were carefully removed from their wood-burning oven. Grain used for these baked goods had come directly from the Mason farm and ground into flour at the local mill. During the summer Clara could look out of her bedroom window and see row after row of toast-colored wheat stalks and the bright green stems and yellow tassels of corn growing in their field.

Men taught their sons how to hunt deer, rabbit, and other animals for meat. Brother Charley was expected to skin the animals, then hang the meat in the barn until it was to be cooked. Roasted chicken for dinner came from the Mason chicken coop. Clara might well have known the name of the chicken whose drumsticks she had for dinner that night!

But there were bigger concerns than just washing clothes and cooking. Farmers had to worry about things that affected how much food they would grow. Would there be enough rain? Is the soil rich enough to grow the season's food for the family, with enough left over to sell as cash crops for a good price? Would insects or birds destroy the harvest?

Now let's take a closer look at what Clara looked like at the time. Here is the complete photo we saw in the beginning at this chapter. We see Clara snuggled by her father's side. While you couldn't tell the time in which she lived by her face alone, now we are able to see some

Clara with her dad

of their 1870s clothing. Notice the starched checkered dress Clara is wearing. It would have been pressed with a heavy iron heated in the fireplace. Imagine ironing on a hot summer day without air conditioning! Before this picture was taken, Clara would have washed in well water gathered in a bucket and carried to the house, instead of turning on a faucet.

Today we are used to modern conveniences. Instant communication through cell phones and the Internet has become a necessity. Fast cars, high-speed trains, and streamlined jets quickly take us anywhere in the world. We multi-task by simultaneously sending text messages while downloading our favorite music and working on homework. Imagine what it was like *not* having any of these conveniences.

In the 1800s, news about the end of a war or the discovery of gold could take weeks or even months. Traveling a hundred miles on horseback could take days, depending on the weather. And think about all the inventions created your lifetime to make life easier, none of which existed at the time.

(left to right) George, Nellie, Nancy, Charley, and Clara

When Clara was seven years old, her father tried to improve life for his family. They relocated to Illinois and continued to farm for the next few years. Clara's father also added to the family income by working as a carriage maker. Since a horse-drawn carriage was as necessary as today's family car, this was definitely a useful second job. The Masons were determined to make a better life, even if it meant moving to a new place and starting over.

Here is a picture of the Mason family from the Illinois days. Notice how children looked like miniature adults, with serious expressions as they pose for their family portrait. The children's clothing is identical to their parents' outfits. For this important event, Nellie might have carefully braided eight-year-old Clara's thick hair, then tied it in a ribbon. Although her lacey collar gives an impression of delicacy, it is in direct contrast to her scuffed shoes, worn out from farm work. Nellie, the twelve-year-old "tween" with her hand on her dad's shoulder, has styled her hair like her mother's, neatly pulled back in a tight bun. Charley at age 17 looks like a grown man, standing dutifully behind his mother and little sister Clara.

Closely observing details in a picture can be a doorway into another time in history. Look carefully at their dad's jacket and you will see a little medal. Are you curious about what it was? So was I. That was why I enlarged the photo to get a closer look. Through some online investigation, I learned that it was a medal from the Civil War, when the North and South fought against each other in the 1860s. After four years of fighting, the North won. Slavery was abolished and the North and South remained a united country. From one small detail in the photograph, we now know that Clara's father fought for the North, because only Northerners were issued these medals. It identified him as a member of the Grand Army of the Republic (G.A.R.), an organization that assisted "Yankee" veterans after the war. After researching his war records I learned Clara's father was injured in battle receiving a gunshot wound to his left leg. Perhaps that was the reason why he wanted to help other veterans, many of whom were wounded in the war. Notice how proudly Clara's father wears both his medal and the gold pocket watch he has tucked into his vest.

It was a big occasion in those days to take a photo like the one we've just seen. Photography was a new invention, so it was costly to have such a memento. Long before the days of phone cameras, the family would have made an appointment with a professional photography

Clara's father wearing his G.A.R. medal

(Courtesy of the Sons of Union Veterans of the Civil War)

studio in town equipped with elaborate props such as carpets, statues, and fancy furniture. For their part, the Masons would have dressed in their best clothes, then stood in the same position in front of the camera for some time—without squirming—before the picture was actually "fixed" with chemicals onto the photographic plate. Next, the photos would be developed and printed by hand.

Here is another photo of Clara from this time period. Instead of posing with her family, she is by herself. The photo gives us a very different look at what a girl of about eight years old might look like. Don't you wonder what Clara was thinking about in this picture? She looks so serious and grown up. I also see a faraway look in her eyes, and I like to think that she was daydreaming about her future. Was she wondering if she would be a farmer's wife and mother like her mom? Did she imagine that one day she would write books or create paintings that would be displayed in a museum? This eight-year-old farm girl in the photo didn't know it at the time, but soon some important events would occur that would change the course of her life.

Chapter Three

Wanted:
Large House with a View
and Spa in Orange County

Imagine being 14 years old, as Clara Mason was in 1887, when your parents decide once again to move, this time more than half a continent away to one of the newest states in America—California! If you were growing up at that time, you would have heard stories of an amazing state bordering the Pacific Ocean, where gold and silver had been discovered and were there for the taking. Maybe you would have heard your parents talking about the U.S. government's description of California as "hundreds of thousands of acres of the finest lands, blest with a climate equal to the fairest portions of Italy." You may have read or heard the words of *New York Tribune* newspaper editor Horace Greeley: "Go West, young man!" You also would have heard about homesteading—a plan that allowed your family to claim free land ownership by filing legal paperwork, living on the land for five years, and making improvements on the property.

Who knew better how to work the land than a family that had proven, both in Ohio and in Illinois, that they could support themselves by farming? So, when the Masons learned about land available for homesteading in California's Orange County, they decided to pack their belongings and once again try to make a better life for themselves.

If you have ever moved a distance, maybe you know how Clara felt leaving all that was familiar. As the Masons boarded the steam locomotive they said good-bye to family and friends with the understanding that they would probably never see each other again. Then, as the train chugged steadily toward their new destination, the Masons may well have had misgivings. Were the pictures they had seen and articles they had read about California really true?

Their anticipation and seeing the Great Plains and Rocky Mountains from their train windows must have heightened the Masons' excitement. The railroad line from San Francisco recently had been extended beyond Los Angeles to San Diego. Both the railroad and the government were encouraging settlers to move to Southern California. The time was right to claim land in or near one of the new towns being built along the railroad route. It must have seemed like an appealing opportunity, especially if you, like Clara, were a bright teenager with big dreams.

This 1897 map of Orange County shows El Toro, just south of Irvine, along the Santa Fe Railroad. Silverado is north of El Toro. Arden, the home of world famous actress Madame Modjeska, is nearby.

Orange County in 1897
(Courtesy of the Orange County Archives)

None of the letters or documents I found told about the Masons' journey to the West. But we do know that travel was much slower than today, when a jet flies from Los Angeles to New York in the time it takes to eat a meal and watch a movie. Other families had come before the Masons, but by covered wagon. The Foxes* were just such a family; they had traveled to California in 1874 by wagon train.

The Santa Fe Railroad first stretched into Orange County, California in 1887, the same year the Masons arrived. We can assume they traveled by train because of that fact. Transportation by railroad was fast replacing travel by horse, stagecoach, and wagon train. What is known for sure from the land records is that the Masons arrived in Orange County, then journeyed to Silverado Canyon, near the base of Saddleback Mountain. They began homesteading on 120 acres. Much of this land was covered with white sage and sweet-smelling wildflowers. What a contrast from the sparse, flat farmland of the Midwest, to find crystal clear streams cascading through a steep canyon, flanked with majestic sycamore and alder trees.

One story about the origins of the Mason's homestead goes like this: When silver was discovered in a piece of ore, more than 300 fortune seekers descended into the area that would become known as Silverado. A stagecoach packed with prospectors arrived one day.

---

*Remember the Fox name, because we will meet this family again—and one Fox in particular will come to play an important part in Clara Mason's life.

Silverado Canyon— Clara's sketch to the left and a photo on the right

The horses were given a break after the long journey, but it apparently wasn't enough for one poor horse named Buck, who decided he would permanently rest in peace at that exact spot. "Buck's tree" became a known monument to the tired old horse that died beneath it on the Mason family's property.

Silverado Canyon might have been sunnier and warmer year round than in Illinois, but living there during the pioneer days wasn't necessarily easier. Once again the Masons needed to be self-reliant if they were going to endure the hardships and isolation of canyon life. Dirt trails connected the canyon residents to a general store some distance away, selling the crucial supplies that everyone needed. But heavy rains would make travel impossible. When the "crick rose," no one could get in or out of the canyon. It would have been too dangerous to travel by horse and wagon through the high waters.

Houses had no running water or flushing toilets; if you were lucky enough to have a kitchen, a pump was primed with water from another location, and the only bathrooms were outhouses. One of Clara's jobs was to carry the harsh-smelling, sulphur water from a spring about a quarter-mile away through the brush and back home. That wasn't the worst of it. We know from a letter that one rainy day, while walking down to the creek, Clara came across a big brown snake. Its markings looked exactly like the dried fern leaves she was walking through. Luckily, Clara had learned about the local plants and animals in school and from her own reading. She immediately identified it as a rattlesnake whose venom might kill her. Slowly backing up, she was able to make a quick getaway toward home!

Another family remembrance from their time in Silverado is about the wild animals that lived in the canyon, not only on the ground, but also in the air. Every mother knew she must keep a watchful eye over her children, even while doing everyday chores such as washing dishes or sweeping the porch. Why? Because grizzly bears and bobcats had been known to lurk nearby in search of food. Plus everyone in Silverado knew about the "big birds" that swooped down and carried away chickens, and some said little children, too. Those "big birds" were California condors weighing up to 25 pounds and having a wingspan of over nine feet. They constantly circled the canyons looking for prey.

California condor
(Courtesy of Jeff Seeman)

Pioneers in Silverado Canyon needed to have the good judgment of a police officer on an emergency call. Always on alert for strange happenings, one winter's evening, while Mr. Mason and Charley were away, Mrs. Mason heard noise coming from the chicken coop. The chickens were nervously clucking and flapping their wings.

Mrs. Mason warned Clara and Nellie to stay in the house while she carefully picked up her shotgun and headed toward the coop to investigate the commotion. They did as they were told and sat close to the fireplace with its soft-glowing embers. Suddenly, a *BANG* resonated through the canyon! Moments later their mother returned to the house. She was shivering not only from the cold, but also from what had just happened. A hungry bobcat had been stalking the chicken coop, and she had killed it.

Clara's mother Nancy Mason on the porch of their home

The next morning, Clara woke at dawn to light a fire in the kitchen stove. The steep canyon walls were holding on tightly to the cold, and morning fog was moving slowly through the trees. Before beginning the day's chores, they looked near the side of the house. There was the dead bobcat, lying frozen on the ground, its fur matted on its lifeless body.

At that moment the family came up with an idea. Together, they dragged the bobcat's lean carcass to the side of the chicken coop and propped it up like a statue against the wall. For the next few days it served as a fine scarecrow to keep other predators away from the chicken coop!

Let's get an idea of what Silverado was like in the early years. A silver mine was located at one end of the canyon and the coal mine, Carbondale, was located on the other end. In 1878, nine years before the Masons arrived, records show there were a number of stores, including two meat markets, offering necessities for the miners and other local residents. At the meat markets, butchers cut slabs of beef and pork raised locally for the miners' wives who stood in line on the sawdust-covered wooden floors, waiting their turn while discussing the latest gossip. Visiting engineers and investors had a place to stay at one of Silverado's three hotels. Horse-drawn carriages pulled up to the entrance where the hotel owner greeted them after their uncomfortable journey from as far away as Los Angeles. In addition, two blacksmith shops were kept busy all hours of the day. Heat blasted from open flames softened the metal to be shaped into tools, machine parts, or horseshoes as the CLANG, CLANG, CLANG of a hammer against an anvil added to the commotion. The most popular establishments were the seven saloons serving whiskey and entertainment to the local miners. It must have been a lively time to live in the canyon!

By 1881 the silver and coal booms were coming to an end and businesses began to close. The nearest city, Orange, was 14 miles away. Santa Ana was a four-hour trip by horseback, and Anaheim was even further. By the time the Mason family homesteaded in 1887, the only signs of habitation to be found in the canyon were a few stone chimneys where buildings had once stood, plus some old shacks scattered on the hillsides. The Masons worked their 120 acres and legally filed their claim to the land. In the early 1890s the government began an investigation to identify homesteaders who were legally entitled to keep their ranches. The Masons and four other families were lucky enough to be granted full rights to their land.

The Soto family, however, was not as fortunate. In 1848 the Mexican government had lost claim to some of their land after the Mexican-American War. Mexico signed a treaty agreeing to give a good portion of their former territory, including California, to the United States. A number of Mexicans and *mestizos*, people of Mexican and Native American descent, remained in the canyons, farming before the homesteaders arrived. The Sotos were one of these families. This original canyon family built a sturdy adobe home with a fireplace and lived there for many years. Because they always had lived on their land, the Sotos thought the land was rightfully theirs and did not file a claim. Eventually the railroad purchased unclaimed land from the government and only the legal homesteaders were allowed to keep their land. Sadly, the Soto family was forced to leave their house and land.

In contrast, the Masons prospered and built one home bigger than the next, until they finally owned one of the grandest homes in the canyon. Clara's early drawings give an idea of what their house looked like.

The Mason family's Silverado Canyon home

Around 1894, a hot sulphur spring was discovered on the Mason family property. Maybe all those buckets of strange-smelling water that Clara carried home for the cooking and washing offered a clue about what was to be found on their property. People believed then, as many still do, that suphur water is a cure for everything from skin problems to stomach ailments. Word spread about the special find on their land. The Masons had the great idea of opening their property to the public. In doing so, they opened the first pioneer spa!

At first people came to visit for the day, as one would go to a day spa today. Those with ailments came to drink and soak in this miraculous water, as well as enjoy the natural beauty of Silverado Canyon. Eventually, the Masons expanded, offering overnight accommodations to visitors from nearby, as well as Los Angeles and Long Beach. Some visitors were local mining engineers. Others traveled a distance to hunt wild animals such as deer and grizzly bears, or to camp out on the land.

Campers in Silverado Canyon
(Courtesy of First American Corporation)

An article from a Santa Ana newspaper, *The Blade*, written around 1896, described a stay at "Mason's Chateau" where one could read and relax or simply enjoy the beautiful surroundings.

Lying full length under the shade of a sycamore tree with a volume of light literature, the air neither cold nor warm, yet so exhilarating, as only pure mountain air can be: the pleasant bubbling and splash of a running brook along the side and arched over which is growing the alder, birch and sycamore, through the openings, occasional glimpses of a sky of deep blue: nothing to do, nothing to think about, with no misgivings of duty unperformed . . . As the place becomes better known there is not the slightest doubt but that Mason's Springs will become one of the most popular resorts in the country.

Gazing up at the blue sky or listening to the brook flowing over the rocks near Mason's Chateau may seem boring. But more than a hundred years ago, appreciating natural beauty was as entertaining as watching a DVD or listening to your favorite playlist while lounging poolside at one of today's five-star resorts. Thanks to this newspaper review, we know Mason's Chateau had become Silverado Canyon's best-known luxury destination.

Chapter Four

Life in the O.C.

Clara was 14 years old when her family moved to Silverado Canyon in Orange County. Here is what Clara looked like when she was about 15 years old.

At the age of 19

In those days, girls would have worn the same outfits until they grew out of them. A dressmaker probably sewed this by hand. First, Clara's measurements would have been taken for a perfect fit. The fabric would have been cut from a huge bolt of cloth and then sewn. Imagine all the work that went into making the ruffles, pleats, and special trimming. Everything was then pressed by hand with an iron heated on the wood-burning kitchen stove. Buttoned or laced-up short leather boots completed the look. They were tight and uncomfortable, unlike today's soft sneakers or cool flip-flops.

What else does Clara's photo show? I think it reveals a young woman with serious thoughts. In addition to her chores, Clara attended school in the City of Orange about fifteen miles from home. She was evolving into an intelligent young woman. Clara loved to learn about her natural surroundings. Silverado became her personal outdoor science camp. While walking the trails of their property she learned to identify the different kinds of rocks including speckled granite, white quartz, and amber-colored agates. She knew every kind of flower and tree that grew in the canyons, both by their popular and scientific names.

Those who knew Clara all agreed that she was an avid reader. To help instill a love of reading in children she gave books as presents for birthdays and Christmas. A number of her sketches portray people reading.

At the age of 19, Clara's love of learning led her to become one of the first, if not the first,

teacher in Silverado Canyon. According to the canyon's librarian and local historian, Clara's classroom was probably a room at a ranch house where one of her students lived. In those days women couldn't marry while they were teaching. However, they could court or date. A young man named Theodore Payne lived nearby. He had emigrated from England to Orange County in 1893 to study California native plants. Soon he landed a job as gardener for the famous actress Madame Helena Modjeska, who lived in the next canyon over from Silverado.

In a book about his experiences in California, Theodore Payne quipped that a person might put on a clean shirt and overalls "to ride over the trail to Silverado Canyon to see the pretty young schoolteacher." Could Theodore Payne have been talking about himself making that trip to visit Clara? We don't know for sure. But we *do* know they both shared a love and interest in plants indigenous to California.

In the 1800s few women had the vision of becoming more than a wife and mother. The belief was that "a woman's place was in the home." Most girls had no more an eighth grade education and few had the opportunity to go on to college. But if

a young woman was smart and had high moral standards she could become a schoolteacher. Teachers did not need formal college level training or a teaching credential at that time. Therefore, teaching was a way for a single woman lacking college training to have a career.

Try to picture Clara as a school teacher with her students in the 1890s. Before the days of cars and school buses, her students saddled up their horses and donkeys to ride on a dirt path to school. Even on wet and cold days students traveled miles to attend Miss Mason's class held in someone's parlor. On warm days, students most likely moved outdoors on benches. Thirsty children needed to carry buckets of water from a nearby spring. No hall passes were required back then to get a drink of water—just dip a cup in the bucket!

Spelling and grammar were taught as soon as a student was able to read. Practicing correct pronunciation meant students needed to read aloud to the teacher every day. Math problems and solutions were written on slate boards with chalk, and then erased to begin the next exercise. Basic math facts, much like today, were memorized in order to solve math problems. Geography lessons consisted of naming, from memory, the locations of places on a globe. Without computers and tools to check spelling and grammar, everything needed to be handwritten perfectly the first time.

Writing was an elaborate process. A quill pen was carefully dipped into an inkwell. Then the student wrote until the ink ran out. The pen was again dipped into the black or blue ink to continue writing. Excess ink was carefully soaked up from the paper with an ink blotter. Correcting a mistake meant crossing out and a big blob of ink might be left on the paper. The teacher might make the student rewrite the entire exercise if that happened.

Not many children lived in the nearby canyons, so young children and teenagers were grouped together to form a class. The littlest ones who had not yet learned to read would be in the same class as the bigger middle school students.

One family had six children attending school. In the middle of the school year, the family decided to move. Their half dozen children made up half of the school's population. The school would have to close if the family moved. So in order to keep the school open, the family decided not to move until the end of the school year.

Among the students attending Clara's class were those from families who had mining claims nearby, as well as children of Mexican descent whose parents worked on local ranches. The students loved their young, pretty, and patient teacher. Clara cared so much about her students that she learned Spanish to be able to communicate with those who couldn't speak English. She became so proficient, in fact, that she wrote some of her poetry in Spanish. This verse is from one of her poems about Laguna Beach that was published in a newspaper.

!De nuevo la brisa salada sentir!
De bondades quiero la una;
Deseo volver y siempre vivir
Acerca del mar en Laguna.

(Oh, to feel once again the salt breeze
o'er the foams
Of joy, give me one, if no other!
I want to return, and to dwell in a home
By the sea in Laguna forever.)

Around the time Clara was teaching, trouble was brewing at home. Clara's parents had drifted apart. A clue to family problems can be seen within their land documents. The ownership of the Silverado Canyon property was listed in Mrs. Mason's name only which was uncommon in those times; land holdings were usually in the husband's name. From the following letter we can tell that Clara's mother not only took care of the Mason household by cooking, but earned an income as well.

Sunday, May 9- '97.
In the Canyon

My Dearest Clara-
I am on guard duty and have just been retrieved to go (make) a good dinner of lima beans, Swiss chard greens with lemon juice, bread and butter, homemade cheese, stewed dried peaches, and strawberries and cream.
- Tea and Jersey (cow) milk
The bees make a lively hum and several hives seem to be on the very verge of sending forth swarms. I got one yesterday and had no trouble whatsoever with them. They were gentle fellows and took to their new home like a duck to water. I have to be constantly on the watch because the hum of work is so loud as to be confusing and sounds like a swarm issuing forth all the time.

She was resourceful when it became necessary to financially support her family. Like many of her neighbors, Mrs. Mason came up with the sweet idea to raise honeybees for income. This was a very clever idea because before sugar was commonly used, honey was the sweetener of choice.

Next to the house, Mrs. Mason had erected an apiary consisting of wooden crates where bees could build their honeycombs. An extracting house allowing the Masons to collect the thick and sweet honey from the honeycombs, stood beside the apiary. A crank spun the round extractor tank, where the honey separated from the combs and collected at the bottom.

Besides providing honey, bees serve another important task. They pollinate flowers on fruit trees. Honey comes in different flavors, depending on which flowers the bees pollinate. Honey might have an essence of lemon, orange, clover, or blueberry.

Pollination insured the Masons an abundance of fruit. In addition, marketing the amber colored honey in Santa Ana proved to be a good business for Clara's mother. She sold the sweetener to stores and farm stands, or bartered it in exchange for other needed items.

Clara's sketch of the apiary and extracting house

The idea of parents separating was something so shameful and unusual at that time that it wasn't openly discussed. In fact in the 1900 census record, Nancy declared herself a widow, rather than admit she and her husband were no longer together. Clara had strong feelings about the marriage commitment. She believed parents should try to work out their problems and stay together. Unfortunately, that is not always possible. If parents cannot work out their differences, rather than argue, they may make the decision to live apart.

Nellie lived with her father for a few years after their parents separated. She met a fine gentleman named Neil McTaggart who eventually would be elected in 1900 to the Orange City Council. On March 6, 1889, *The Orange News* included among its announcements that "N.G. McTaggart, well and favorably known in Orange, will marry Nellie Mason of El Modena this evening at the home of her father, G.W. Mason."

In time, Neil and Nellie had three children: Raymond, Ralph, and Marguerite, who was nicknamed Marge. All five McTaggarts are shown in this photo along with Clara, and Clara and Nellie's mother Nancy.

(Back row, standing) brother-in-law Neil McTaggart and 21 year old Clara (Front row) Clara's sister Nellie with her sons, Raymond (age 5) and Ralph (age 3), next to Clara's mother, holding 5-month-old Marguerite (Marge) on her lap

Even though Charley, her "loving big brother" (as he referred to himself), worked far from home, he kept in touch with Clara through visits and letters. Charley held some unusual jobs, such as selling sheet music door-to-door and building booths for the annual Parade of Products. It was a combination street and county fair, first held in celebration of the new electric Red Cars that linked Los Angeles, Orange, Ventura, and San Bernardino counties.

With her siblings gone, Clara was left to support her mother through some difficult times. But, as is often the case, by overcoming hardships she became more courageous and resilient. For Clara, drawing and painting served as a distraction from her sadness for a long time. Many of us know a favorite place where we can escape from everything. It may be your bedroom, the beach, or the mall. Clara worked through her pain by escaping to the winding canyon trail near her home, with sketchbook and pencils in

"Huckleberry."

"Huckleberry

hand. By concentrating on drawing the rugged mountains, meandering brooks, and gentle calves grazing on their property, her problems melted away… at least for a while.

Animals were some of Clara's favorite subjects. One in particular was their cat Huckleberry. Every day he visited the houses along the road and became an expert in knowing which served the best meals. Full and satisfied after a feast of leftovers, Huckleberry would return home and curl himself into a ball, then slumber on the porch in the warm sunlight. He was unaware that while asleep, he had become a perfect model for Clara's sketches!

By the time Clara was 22 years old, she made a very important decision. As much as she loved Silverado, the young woman desired to expand her horizons as well as sharpen her artistic skills. Seeing her parents drift apart had been heartbreaking. This would be the perfect time for Clara to leave home for a while to focus her creative energies rather than dwell on her parents' separation. So she decided, after much thought, to continue her education in far away New York City.

An assortment of children and furry creatures were the inspiration for these sketches

It couldn't have been easy to find a way to fulfill her dreams. The Victorian Era of the late 1800s was a time when few acceptable jobs were available to women. As a woman, Clara was expected to marry, stay home, and raise a family. Most young women in Silverado, El Toro, and other communities were married when they were in their teens. As for education, few girls attended high school and even fewer went on, as Clara did, to receive a higher level of education.

Clara thought differently. Although she was a soft-spoken person, she didn't think a woman was a second-class citizen —even in those days, when women were not yet allowed to vote. Clara believed she could achieve whatever she put her mind to doing. And what she wanted to do was to study art.

Clara had heard about New York City's Cooper Union. The school was built on the dream of giving gifted people a chance to develop their talents. Clara learned that all qualified students who were creative thinkers with a talent in art or science could receive full-tuition scholarships. Innovative minds such as Thomas Edison, inventor of the light bulb, had attended Cooper Union. A number of presidents, including Barack Obama, have presented speeches in Cooper Union's great auditorium. In 1860 Abraham Lincoln's oration on the evils of slavery could have been heard at the school's hall for an admission fee of 25 cents.

Clara Mason knew that attending an outstanding school such as Cooper Union would give her a strong foundation in art, as well as a time away from home. She applied and was accepted. How excited she must have been to receive the letter telling her so!

Just 20 years prior, America's last track had been laid for the transcontinental railroad connecting the east and west coasts by train. And that is how it happened that in the year 1896, Clara Mason, young pioneer woman, boarded a northbound train from the El Toro depot to Los Angeles. A connecting train then took her to San Francisco where she boarded yet another train. Six days after leaving El Toro, she had arrived in New York City. Clara's friends and family must have been astonished by the thought of this determined young woman—unmarried and unaccompanied by any male family members—traveling cross-country to New York.

A new adventure had certainly begun!

Chapter Five

Great Expectations for Clara

At different times, Clara and I both lived in the same city. Clara lived in New York City while attending school at Cooper Union for the Advancement of Science and Art. I grew up in New York City, and for me, it will always be home.

Some say, "Once a New Yorker, always a New Yorker." I believe it. As a child I lived in a world of towering buildings, flashing neon store signs, and lots of people. Cars and taxis maneuvered as if they were on a racetrack. The din of jackhammers and horns created the background music for New York's urban setting. My family lived in an apartment within a cluster of seven-story high housing project buildings on 14th Street. I felt secure knowing we were just a holler away from the family who lived next door to us. Even better, there was no shortage of kids when I wanted to play stoopball or hopscotch.

Saturdays were spent walking through Central Park or viewing the golden Prometheus statue from the railing at Rockefeller Center while skaters whirled on the ice below. Every year I eagerly anticipated the spectacular Christmas and Easter shows at Radio City Music Hall. The skyscrapers, Fifth Avenue, and world-class museums are large-than-life to visitors, but to me, New York City was simply *home*.

Clara came from a very different life experience than mine. In contrast, she grew up on isolated farms and in a canyon with towering trees and dirt trails. Clara needed to get her mind off the problems going on at home. New York City served as a welcomed diversion.

A short time before her parents married, Clara's mother Nancy received a letter cautioning her about her husband-to-be, George. I came across the letter in Clara's belongings found in the attic. It was written by Nancy's brother during the Civil War from Camp Sherman. He had known George for many years. Although no specific reason was given, he implied that George was not the marrying kind and would not make a good husband.

Nancy, however, was in love and married him in spite of the warning. And in the earlier years of their marriage, things seemed to work out. In the beginning they made a home in Ohio and raised their three children, then later moved to Illinois. Upon moving to Silverado Canyon, Nancy continued to maintain a comfortable home for her husband and three children. Maybe she kept her sadness hidden all along to keep the family together.

Clara loved her mother and was close to her father, too. This is evident in the photos showing Clara leaning on his shoulder or holding on tightly to his sleeve. He was undeniably a hardworking man, laboring as a farmer, carriage maker, and businessman to provide his family with all the necessities. Yet he and Nancy were not happy together. Nearly 3,000 miles from home Clara must have had the lingering thought that her father would not be there when she returned to Silverado. New York is certainly a place where a person can get lost in a crowd or distracted enough—at least for a while—to forget one's troubles.

I close my eyes and try to imagine how Clara felt arriving at Grand Central Depot in New York, the nation's largest city at the time. The rumbling of the incoming steam locomotive as it slowly screeched to a stop and exhaled one last puff, would have carried vibrations throughout the terminal. Instead of balancing on step stones across the cool creek waters or standing alone in the stillness of the canyon, Clara stepped off the colossal locomotive onto a concrete platform, then moved along with the masses of people who were making their way through the train station.

Light streaming through enormous arched windows on marble walls would have added to Clara's disorientation and amazement. The vast open space in the center of the concourse served as the grand entrance, welcoming visitors to New York City. The crowning jewel of the Main Concourse was a four-faced, gold-toned clock. She had never experienced crowds of people like those criss-crossing the terminal to get to their trains on time, feeling similar to today's mall crowds on the first official shopping day of the Christmas season!

A blare of announcements for trains departing to Philadelphia, Chicago, and Boston would have been heard as passengers pressed toward their destinations. Friends and family rushed to greet those who had just disembarked their trains. But no one was waiting at the depot to welcome Clara. She was alone and trying to find her way to the street level. Signs pointed the way to Park Avenue and 42nd Street. She tried to figure out which direction to go.

There probably was a moment when she stopped, took a deep breath, briefly closed her eyes, and—realizing she was alone and almost 3,000 miles away from home—hoped everything would turn out the way she had planned. As she walked the ramp and onto the street level, the clattering of horses' hooves on cobblestone, the honking of streetcar horns, and shouts of street vendors must have astonished this pioneer girl who was accustomed to the quiet and calmness of Silverado Canyon.

Pedestrians needed to pay attention when crossing streets during this time of transition in the city's transportation. Shiny new electric streetcars whisked passengers to destinations across town and over bridges to outlying areas. Horses left their manure on the pavement as they pulled carriages full of passengers to their destinations. One had to step carefully when crossing the street.

Beggars sat on sidewalks reaching out for a few coins from passers by. Peddlers with their pushcarts called out, "Ho, here are fresh carrots, corn, and string beans!"

New York, in all its excitement and newness, must have demanded Clara's com-

plete attention, while thoughts of Orange County faded from her mind. Instead of hiking through the steep rocky canyons of Silverado, she now wandered the city's canyons of wood, brick, and stone buildings, looming up to ten stories high. Today, the few nineteenth century buildings that remain are dwarfed by modern New York City structures more than one hundred stories high.

1890s New York City Map
(PD-US)

62 Perry Street, New York City

Clara made her way to the West Village where a maple tree-lined street of brownstone apartment buildings would be her new home. Perry Street was known for the many artists and poets who resided there. A flight of steps led her to a wooden arched doorway bearing the number 62. Clara's apartment was located on the second floor of the building, giving her a bird's eye view of the activity below.

From her tall parlor window facing Perry Street, she could look down and watch the constant motion of people moving like bees around their hives back in Silverado. On one wall was a grand fireplace with a rectangular gilded-framed mirror above it. In the evening, the looking glass reflected the sparkle of candles and kerosene lamps positioned on the fireplace mantel.

Outside was a lively neighborhood with art galleries and shops as well as a busy stable down the street. Passengers arriving at Perry Street by horse-drawn vehicles, stepped onto a small wooden stool from their high carriages to the sidewalk. A black iron street lamp stood at the corner and illuminated the curb.

Each evening as the sun set, a lamplighter ignited the streets' kerosene-fueled lights one by one, like birthday candles on a cake. Using his ladder and a pole with a wick on the end, he reached inside the hinged doors of the lamps and lit the wicks of the flickering gaslights. Although the gas company paid him for his work, the lamplighter paid for the matches with his own money. That meant each time he lit a wick, he was careful to quickly close the lamp door. Otherwise, if a breeze swept by and extinguished the flame, he would have to relight

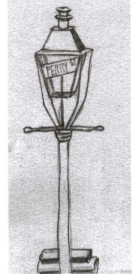

Lamppost and wooden stepstool

a blown-out lamp using another one of his own matches. His was truly an important job, since he also served as a neighborhood watchman on the lookout for thieves and prowlers. Then before the sun rose over the awakening city, the lamplighter would retrace his steps, extinguishing each lamp. The quiet of dawn would be broken as rattling, horse-pulled milk carts made their way down residential streets, delivering fresh milk to apartment residents.

In the morning, instead of the cool fresh canyon air of Silverado, Clara awoke to a mixture of city smells. The stench of manure from horse stables and belching odors from factories and breweries were layered with the perfume of flowers sold from pushcarts and wafting aromas of food cooking from nearby apartments. On her way to school, about 14 blocks away, Clara walked streets lined with restaurants selling delicacies she probably never had tasted, such as freshly shucked oysters from Long Island Sound, grilled flounder and halibut caught in the nearby sea-green Atlantic waters, and homemade pastas served with crusty Italian bread. What better way to start the day than with an omelet, warm rolls, and a hot cup of coffee, all for only 10 cents,

at a cozy neighborhood diner? Immigrants who recently arrived from Italy, Hungary, and Greece, as well as many other European countries, could be heard speaking their native languages at nearby tables.

It must have all been overwhelming. We can even see some of Clara's uneasiness in several of her first sketches. Like a tourist, she captured "snapshots" of her new environment through drawings that appear to be unfinished, concentrating on simple outlines without much detail. It would take persistence, devotion to her studies, and a growing sense of comfort in her surroundings before Clara began to develop a sense of mastery in her artwork.

Cooper Union operated much like a work-study program does today. Students were encouraged to earn a living while attending school. Morning classes allowed students time in the afternoon for jobs that trained them in art-related fields of interest. Some students worked in advertising or as apprentices for designers. Others gave art lessons for a fee. One of the goals of Cooper Union was to bring together employers and talented students who might become their future employees.

It was of equal importance for students to develop good character as well as acquire the skills needed for success at school. Cooper Union was known for training students to become not only skilled artists, but responsible citizens who could make good decisions. Such characteristics were taken into consideration when recommending a pupil for a job. Students had to work hard, and not everyone was able to complete their studies. If a pupil did not show seriousness and good effort, she was asked to leave the school. In fact, the year when Clara attended Cooper Union more than 500 students applied for the school year, but only 265 were accepted. Less than 200 of those accepted were able to complete their coursework and eventually graduate.

Clara attended the Woman's Art School at Cooper Union. Classes for men and women were separate. The female student population had increased by nearly 300 in 20 years, since more women were attending college and earning degrees. And unlike college today, only students ranging in age from 16 to 35 could attend.

Clara's morning classes focused on learning to draw in pen and ink, pencil, and charcoal. Course titles included 'Drawing from the Antique,' 'Drawing from Life,' 'Perspective,' 'Cast Drawing,' 'Pen and Ink Illustration,' 'Oil Painting,' 'Crayon Photographs,' and 'Photo Color and Retouching.' Like the others, Clara worked in the afternoons, probably teaching art to younger students or as an assistant to other artists, where she could use her talents as well as earn some spending money.

Students listened intently to professors giving lectures on 'Design' or 'Anatomy' that focused on drawing the human form. Students learned about

Model Selene Dorch with doll

Pencil sketch

Pen and ink drawing

Charcoal drawing

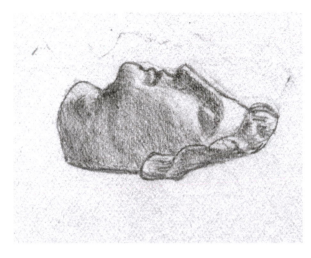

then-contemporary American artists such as Mary Cassatt and Claude Monet, the daring new French Impressionist. On Saturday evenings, free art lectures were held on campus and open to the public. Topics included 'China and the Chinese' and 'Evolution of Society' to satisfy the increasingly popular interests at that time in world cultures and travel.

Through practice, the guidance of her teachers, and encouragement from her classmates and friends, Clara's artistic skills reached new levels. In her 'Drawing From the Antiques' class, Clara sketched statue reproductions from well-known sculptors such as Michelangelo, as well as from live models. In those days statues and models were fully clothed or draped for modesty, keeping private parts of the body *private*!

We know how our friends can be sympathetic listeners and give us inspiration. Clara had her group of friends, too. They even made up a nickname for themselves: "The Spread." She found this group of friends—among them, Carl Bond, Polly Oliver, Cora Junks, and Ellen Freeman—to be compatible and supportive as those who were students busily worked together on school assigned projects. They undoubtedly discussed their concerns about maintaining good grades as well as the frustration of having to redo a rejected drawing until it met with their teacher's approval. It is tempting to imagine "The Spread" complaining about too much homework or excitedly discussing what they were going to do on the weekend.

With the companionship of friends, Clara began to feel at ease in the city. It was no longer an unfamiliar place to be feared. She frequently corresponded with her mother sharing her feelings and what was going on in her life. Since social networking would not be available for another hundred years, Clara dipped her pen into an inkwell to handwrite her letters. After a few months in the city she wrote this observation to her mother: "New York actually seems small to me now. At first it

New York actually seems small to me now. At first it was immense, noisy and bewildering, and I dreaded every street crossing and attempt at finding a new place. But New York is laid out so simply, folks, men and signs are everywhere and familiarity breeds contempt. Of course I suppose there are dangers but what you need is to keep your eyes open and tend your own business.

was immense, noisy and bewildering, and I dreaded every street crossing. . . . But New York is laid out so simply, policemen and signs are everywhere. . . ." However, when Clara added, "Familiarity breeds contempt," she meant that when you get to know something or someone well, you find their flaws. In this case, Clara eventually learned that if a person doesn't look out for herself and to what is going on, the city could be a dangerous place.

An envelope containing a letter sent from Orange, California, on May 11, 1897

Clara's letters to her mother also give us a sense of her social life when she wasn't in class. One letter in particular gives us insight into plans she made with girlfriends.

So it seems that like most young women, Clara and her girlfriends "dressed to impress" by showing off their new hats at church. The fashionistas must have had fun shopping together in department stores such as Macy's and John Wanamaker & Company. Shops serving coffee and pie were very popular and, like today's Starbuck's, they were located throughout the city. It's easy to

Brooklyn Bridge connecting Manhattan to Brooklyn

picture the girls going for a quick coffee break on nearby Bleeker Street, then—on their way home—peeking between buildings for a view of the newly completed Brooklyn Bridge as well as New Jersey across the Hudson River.

Although Clara was now feeling at home in New York, she knew that soon she must return home to California. The end of the school year came on Thursday, May 27, 1897 with the Annual Reception for the Woman's Art School. Sadly, neither of her parents attended the ceremony, although she had been given two tickets for them. Traveling from California to New York would have been a long journey for Nancy and George. More importantly, the situation would have been awkward, since they were no longer living together. Clara's graduation reminded her once again that her parents were separated. All

Cooper Union
for the Advancement of Science and Art.

Thirty-eighth Annual Reception of the
Woman's Art School,

Thursday Evening, May 27th, 1897
at eight o'clock.

R. Swain Gifford,
Art Director

Abram S. Hewitt,
Secretary.

Mary A. Vinton,
Principal.

Admit Gentleman and Ladies.

Ticket to the Woman's Art School's Annual Reception held on May 27, 1897

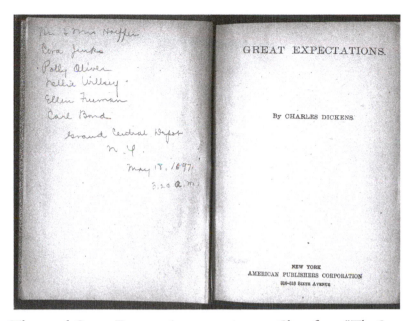

*The novel **Great Expectations** was given to Clara from "The Spread"*

the same, she held on to their tickets and brought them home to California as a keepsake. Then she placed them in a box with some other papers. They would not be found for more than a hundred years.

Knowing that her parents would not be able to attend, Clara left for home on May 18, more than a week before the art school celebration was to take place. She and her good friends, "The Spread," got together one last time at Grand Central Depot, where Clara had first arrived months earlier in New York. Grand Central Station with its tall marble columns and huge arched windows was the perfect dramatic backdrop for their final good-byes. Wishing their former classmate well, "The Spread" helped Clara with her baggage, sketchbooks, and mementos in hand and watched her as she boarded her train.

Just before Clara parted from her friends, "The Spread" gave her a copy of Charles Dickens' *Great Expectations*. Originally, the novel was published between 1860 and 1861 as a series of stories, appearing in a magazine one chapter at a time. Today, this book is considered a classic along with *Huckleberry Finn* and *Little Women. Great Expectations!* What a perfect book title for a person about to begin the next chapter of her life. As the train left and Clara looked back one last time, she must have had conflicting thoughts. Leaving the friends she made and the city she had come to enjoy, had to have been difficult. At the same time, Clara must have anticipated returning home to California with her developed artistic skills to record the impressions of such places as Silverado Canyon and Laguna Beach.

Chapter Six

Home Again

It was May of 1897 when Clara arrived home to Silverado Canyon. Her mother's parlor window framed yellow bursts of Chinese lilies as they "consented to bloom in the bright sunlight of spring." The bees in the apiary "made a perfect hum as they worked strongly together," according to Clara's mother. As if these were signs of hope, Clara felt content to be home again. Her mother welcomed Clara's companionship as well as her help, especially with the apiary. Extracting honey from the combs and delivering it to markets in Santa Ana and Anaheim was time consuming. As for Clara's father, we know from an 1896 newspaper article that he had been living further inland from Silverado, in the community of Moreno, since his separation from Nancy.

Clara undoubtedly looked forward to the little spare time she could find to take out her sketchbook and pencils to draw, or to sit by a creek and think about her time in New York City and what her life held in store, now that she had returned home.

The nineteenth century was coming to a close. New inventions, such as the sewing machine, telephone, and electric light bulb were making life easier. And new inventions also led to new ways of thinking. The "New Woman" wanted more rights. Only after years of struggle known as Women's Suffrage did women finally gain the legal right to vote in 1920, through the passage of the 19th Amendment to the Constitution. Women also came together to fight for better educational advantages and employment opportunities.

Clara was not one to march with a picket sign or give speeches for women's rights. Her way of expressing her thoughts was through art and writing, as well as participation in community organizations.

Later in life, she served as secretary of her local P.E.O. (Philanthropic Educational Organization) chapter. The P.E.O. was a new organization aimed at improving educational opportunities for women that, to this day, provides scholarships and loans to further women's education. As a former teacher, Clara was well aware that a good education empowers people to succeed in the careers of their choice.

Clara was an intelligent woman and a deep thinker. But like most of us, she took time for relaxation and fun. When temperatures rose into the 80s and the dry, scorching winds of Silverado blew like a blast of heat from a hot oven, the 18-mile journey west to Laguna Beach was worth the trip. Most traveled to Laguna by way of the El Toro stagecoach. Clara's family, however, owned a horse and buggy for just such excursions.

The four-hour ride began along Santiago Canyon with a turn on El Toro Road. At the end of El Toro Road, vacationers turned west onto Laguna Canyon Road that ended at Main Beach. The bumpy ride transported passengers past rolling hills with outcroppings of majestic boulders. Sycamore and oak trees washed in golden sunlight dotted the hillsides. Kicked-up dust mingled with the scent of sage as the horses continued on to Laguna. To the east, the evening summer sky was a watercolor wash of pink and azure streaks with violet shadows folding across Saddleback Mountain in the distance.

The worst aspect of the trip was that the route was known to be a target for holdups.

A stagecoach travels along Laguna Canyon Road in 1898 (Courtesy of Bowers Museum)

Sections of the road were sandy, so the horses needed to travel at a slower pace. It was at these hollows that bandits would strike, then run for the hills. The surrounding caves that cut into the boulders made perfect hideouts for outlaws until the next group of unsuspecting travelers made their way down the road. Fortunately, Clara always managed to get to her destination unscathed without encountering bandits. Despite the long journey and occasional hold-ups, Laguna had become a popular place for visitors from inland towns and Los Angeles.

Watercolor of John J. Seeman's house at Arch Beach painted by Mary F. Bradshaw

Laguna's population swelled every June through August as visitors sought relief from the summer heat, and enjoyed the cool coastal breezes. Since few hotels existed in Laguna, many vacationers set up tents along the shore and cliffs. However, once summer ended, Laguna reverted back to being a quiet beach town with few year-round residents.

In 1886 a home lot could be purchased at Arch Beach (now Pearl Street) for $75. Back then people were practical. Wooden houses along the cliffs had small windows to keep out the chilly night breezes. They weren't concerned with having an ocean view. After all, why would anyone want to look at the ocean through a window when the beach was just a short walk away? Today, oceanfront homes at Pearl Street take full advantage of the ocean air, and homeowners pay millions of dollars to have whitewater

Clara's drawing of Arch Beach

Arch Beach in the late 1800s
(Courtesy of First American Corporation)

Beach house window sill

Arch Beach house

Wading in a tide pool, 1899
(Courtesy of Bowers Museum)

Laguna Beach bathers in 1890 (Courtesy of Bowers Museum)

and Catalina Island views. Most houses have large glass sliding doors and windows to feel the same breezes the early settlers wanted to keep out, and to enjoy the spectacular panoramas. How times have changed!

Clara's beach days were devoted to collecting shells, such as iridescent abalone and tiny brown coffee shells, as she walked along the shoreline. Tide pools at "The Arch" rock formation resembled water gardens filled with swaying kelp, crabs moving like wind-up toys, and spiny sea urchins. Indigo blue mussels clinging to the rocks, were gathered by the locals and boiled in big pots to make a tasty dinner. Locally grown lima beans, ripe red tomatoes, and slices of sweet juicy watermelon completed the meal.

Without air conditioning or electric lights, people spent most of their time outdoors. Fishing, walking along the shore, or playing in the sand was fun, but when the sun rose high in the afternoon sky, napping on the porch became a favorite diversion. Feeling the refreshingly misty ocean breezes while being lulled to sleep with the rhythmic sounds of waves was a perfect way to spend a warm summer afternoon.

John J. Seeman's house at Arch Beach (Courtesy of First American Corporation)

On a calm day, slight ripples on the water revealed thousands of silvery sardines below the surface. Plump lobsters were there for the taking, just a short boat row away. Drifting in a wooden skiff or bobbing buoyantly on the rolling waves were also popular pastimes on a sunny summer morning. Youngsters liked going barefoot as they made their way down a cliff to the beach. Fish were so plentiful they could be caught by hand in the waves and tide pools.

The beach scene was very different from today. People dressed modestly during the Victorian Era. Girls wore full-length dresses and big bonnets to shield their faces from the

sun. Boys wore woolen shirts and shorts. There were no umbrellas, beach chairs, or sun block. Swimmers struggled coming out of the water in their long woolen swim outfits. Then they dried off by stretching out in the sand in their soggy salty swimsuits. What would people from those times have thought about the bikinis and board shorts we wear at the beach these days?

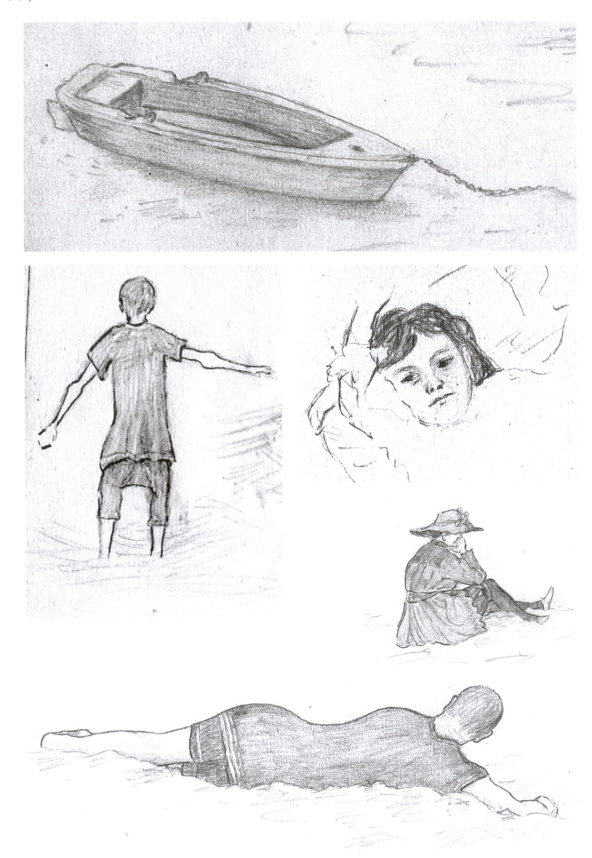

Clara's sense of humor is obvious in these captions of a man experiencing "a partial eclipse" under his hat and the one-legged "crane" wading into the water.

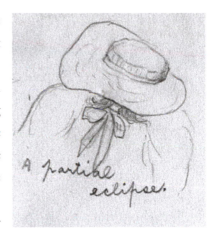

Clara was never far from her pencils and sketchpad while at the beach. She loved observing people and drawing even the smallest details. Today, Clara is recognized as one of Laguna Beach's first artists. Her drawings give us some of the earliest glimpses of what Laguna Beach sunbathers looked like and how they dressed.

Even though Laguna was a paradise for water activities, water also was a real problem for its residents. Not much was available for drinking. Big buckets of water needed to be filled from a pump for cooking and washing. A water pump was located on Laguna Canyon Road, about a mile north of Arch Beach. Another was at Aliso Canyon, two miles south. The alternative was to purchase a barrel of water for about 50 cents from a water wagon. Another inconvenience was the lack of indoor plumbing; outhouses were the only toilets. And without access to electricity, the dim light of candles and kerosene lanterns appeared each evening from beach cottage windows.

In the summertime, a butcher passed through town once a week, providing fresh cuts of meat for the vacationers. Laguna also had a local baker and milkman, and a barber made his rounds every two weeks, a sort of mobile groomer providing haircuts and shaves. People from outlying cities especially seemed to enjoy the slower, simpler lifestyle in Laguna, along with balmy summer weather.

Just about this time, dramatic scenery accompanied by a distinctive natural light was attracting artists from far away places. This excerpt from poetry by Clara describes the artists who set up their easels along the sides of the roads.

The Laguna Painters

And when you pass, on either hand
The busy painters you will see;
Upon the cliffs, upon the sand,
Their wide umbrella-ed easels stand,
And there they work engrossedly.
Upon the sea with gaze intent,
Then from the range of rainbow hues
Some bits of color they will choose,
To be upon their pallets blend.

Today, artists continue to paint the same vistas of the cliffs, shores, and ocean.

Besides watching the painters and locals of Laguna Beach, Clara began noticing someone who lived right in her own backyard—or close to it! Do you recall, earlier in this book, when I suggested you remember the name Fox of Silverado Canyon? Well, now you will find out why.

Clara had known George Fox for years. His parents were homesteaders like the Masons in nearby Bell Canyon. George's family arrived in California from Texas by wagon train on the Butterfield Stagecoach Route passing through El Paso and Fort Yuma. They too were beekeepers, aptly naming their home Bee Ranch and marketing their honey in Santa Ana, the nearest city. The one-time site of Bell Canyon Ranch is now part of the National Audubon Society's Starr Ranch Sanctuary, dedicated to environmental education as well as preserving rare animal habitats.

In the fall of 1898, George had returned home to Bell Canyon Ranch after serving as a soldier with the Seventh California Infantry in the Spanish-American War. Trained in San Francisco for the military, George was prepared to serve his country by fighting Spain after the February 1898 sinking of the U.S. battleship *Maine*. As it turned out, the United States proved to be a world power in a war that lasted less than 100 days. A peace treaty ended the war before George's unit was called into combat. Thankfully, he returned home safely to both his family and his sweetheart, Clara.

While Clara's days were kept busy at the Silverado home with her drawing, writing, and visits to Laguna Beach, she also made time to become better acquainted with her neighbor. George was a strong, good-looking man with a friendly smile. He stood 5 feet 8 inches, had dark brown eyes, and thick wavy hair combed neatly in place. His initiative and physical strength were necessary for the strenuous work that was available at the time. Fields and hills were being prepared for development. George and his brother were among those grading the land with mule teams and heavy equipment in areas as diverse as Newport Beach, Los Angeles, and Bakersfield. He wisely invested his income from this work in the purchase of Aliso Canyon land.

Long hours of work in the fields gave George a good appetite. Some say the way to man's heart is through his stomach, and George was no exception, especially when it came to Clara's cooking. We can imagine Clara preparing a hearty dinner of pot roast, ripened tomatoes, and homemade bread with preserves. The dinner would have been served at a candlelit table near the kitchen. After the meal they may have retreated to the parlor, playing popular songs like "Yankee Doodle" and "My Wild Irish Rose" on the organ. Or perhaps they went horseback riding on nearby canyon trails at dusk. Conversations might have gradually turned to the latest book Clara had read or about mutual plans for the future. Their love for each other continued to deepen. George and Clara were drawn to each other... like bees to honey!

George became attracted to Clara's finer qualities. According to J.E. Pleasants' *History of Orange County*, the first teachers in Orange County were described as "intelligent, upright, courageous, with a sense of responsibility to the community." That certainly sums up Clara very well.

The couple courted, or dated, for a number of years. Most girls in those days were married by their late teens. But Clara was 33, the same age as George, when he asked, "Will you marry me?" And of course she said, "Yes!" Did Clara wait until she was older because she feared having an unhappy marriage like her parents? Perhaps. But finally she was sure as could be that she wanted to spend the rest of her life with her longtime sweetheart. By the time they married on June 1, 1905, in Los Angeles County, both were ready to start the next chapter of their lives together as husband and wife.

George and Clara

Chapter Seven

Together Wherever

After their marriage in 1905, Clara and George relocated wherever he could find work. Their first home was a ranch in Aliso Canyon not far from Silverado. But soon they heard about the need for men to work in the newly discovered oil fields of Los Angeles.

The story goes that in 1892 Edward Doheny discovered oil by accident. He noticed the dark, gooey substance on the wheel of a cart and followed its track back to Echo Park. Next, he made wise investment by purchasing the Echo Park property, making him a wealthy man. Soon 2,500 wells sprang up on Los Angeles hillsides like bean sprouts on fertile soil, making the city one of the richest oil producing regions on the planet. Just as the Gold Rush and the lure of silver mines had attracted people to California 50 years earlier, the oil fields fueled employment for energetic young workers such as George.

So, George and Clara left Orange County and moved to the growing city of Los Angeles. George's family remained in Silverado. However, Clara's mother Nancy could no longer take care of the Silverado property by herself. Nancy sold

George, Clara's mother Nancy, and Clara

what was left of the home's contents to move in with Clara and George.

It is interesting to look at property values at the time and compare them to today's costs, when California homes sell for millions of dollars and we pay thousands of dollars for new furniture. The 1899 tax records kept at the Orange County Archives show these assets from the Silverado property:

furniture	$30
organ	$10
wagon	$5
2 horses	$30
cow	$15
beehives	$25

Thirty-five dollars for a wagon and two horses! Today, a car can cost a thousand times that amount.

Sadly, in 1915 Clara's father died in a veterans' hospital at the age of 72. Three years later, her mother passed away at the age of 76. Clara mourned the loss of her parents who had been living apart for years. But with the support of her husband, she moved past her grieving and into a time of great creativity. Once again, she channeled her loss and sadness into artistic energy. Her days were spent painting and writing. She created so many paintings that she generously gave them away to friends and neighbors. Today, only two of her paintings can be located.

Her first book of poetry, In Pleasant Places, was published in 1924. She received recognition when several of her poems appeared in the *Los Angeles Times* newspaper. Clara had the ability to use words as though they were a palette of paint colors expressing her joy of life and spirituality in nature. Here is an excerpt from her poem titled "Laguna Painters."

And when your coloring is done,
The real painting ye have but begun.
For God has worked this fair design
With more than color, more than line,
For he has painted, too, with wind and sun
The light, the glow, and salty air,
Sea-flavored: yea.

As if Clara had not expressed herself enough through her art and poetry, she took on a new assignment: designing a house for her adored niece, Marguerite (nicknamed Marge), the daughter of Clara's sister Nellie and husband Neil McTaggert. Since George and Clara were childless, they had a special fondness for their nephews and nieces. By the mid 1920s, Marge had married Ed Seeman, Laguna's first fire chief. Following Clara's architectural

Marge and Ed's home at 1796 Glenneyre in Laguna Beach

plans, their Craftsman-style home was built at 1796 Glenneyre in Laguna Beach. It was there that Marge and Ed raised a family and lived out their lives.

The Craftsman bungalow with stone walls and chimney had become a popular style of architecture in the early years of the twentieth century. Marge and Ed's house is described in the Laguna Beach City Hall land records as a "Craftsman house with box plan, multi-gabled roof and shingle siding." It had "multi-paned windows" adorning the south corner, with "an ocean stone retaining wall" extending "across the front of the lot." Stones from the Sierra Mountains were used "to form meandering pathways" to a garden of morning glories and fragrant white freesia in back of the house. The city land record ends with this sentence: "The house was designed by Marguerite's aunt, Clara Mason Fox, artist and author of *A History of El Toro*." It was in the attic of this house that Clara's belongings were found decades later.

The familiarity and charm of the Saddleback Valley lured Clara and her husband George back to the area they loved so much. In 1930 they moved again, purchasing a tract of land in El Toro (known today as Lake Forest), about ten miles from Silverado Canyon.

George and Clara's home in El Toro

Their picture-perfect house was built in El Toro near Cherry Street and Second Avenue close to the Bennett family home. The Fox's home was similar in design to the Bennett's ranch house, with a stone fireplace and chimney. A barn stood next to the house. Trees bearing walnuts, oranges, and plump apricots grew on the Fox property, supplying them with plenty of nuts and fresh fruit. Eucalyptus trees provided wood for their fireplace and kitchen stove.

Close your eyes and imagine the fragrance of orange blossoms and the feel of a cool breeze in the shade of a sage-green eucalyptus tree. You are refreshed, sipping a glass of slightly tart, fresh-squeezed lemonade while swinging on a hammock. Clucking chickens, the soft whiny of a horse, along with the occasional lowing of a cow, all roaming freely on the ranch, provide a comforting lullaby of sounds.

Their cow gave fresh milk and cream that was hand-churned into butter. The ample supply provided plenty for the couple and enough to share with neighbors. Dairy products were stored in a cupboard near the cellar with wire shelves allowing the cooler air to circulate—something necessary before the days of refrigerators.

Clara added her special creative touches to the home with some unusual souvenirs collected on a trip. She and George had taken a six-month journey by horse and buggy to Yosemite, stopping to visit relatives along the way. The new national park in California was drawing the attention of artists, poets, and photographers.

As the couple traveled through the park in their horse-drawn buggy, they gazed in amazement at the glacial features, such as majestic El Capitan and the mighty Merced River that flowed swiftly through the Yosemite Valley. They made sure to stop along the way and collect unusual rocks. When it came time to build the El Toro house, Clara transformed their Yosemite rock collection along with other rocks, into a unique fireplace that served as the focal point of their living room. A stone pestle Clara had found, once used by the local Native Americans to grind acorns, was cemented into the fireplace as a convenient holder for matches. Her artwork decorated the walls and kitchen tiles of the cozy Fox home.

El Capitan in Yosemite National Park
(Courtesy of Barbara Price)

Here is something interesting about Clara's art: she never used bright red in her landscape paintings. Perhaps she thought of red as a harsh color. Her interest was in representing the beauty of God's creation. That meant using muted earth tones such as azure blue, olive green, deep amethyst, and yellow ochre.

The community of El Toro in rural Saddleback Valley consisted primarily of farmers who formed a closely-knit community. Friends and neighbors helped each other in time of need, whether it was to repair a fence or help a widow harvest the year's crops. Before TV, computers, and skateboard parks, El Toro's Community Hall was the happening place for entertainment. Bonding among neighbors grew even stronger when they socialized at the Community Hall.

El Toro Community Hall
(Courtesy of the Heritage Hill Historical Society)

These gatherings were a way to say "thanks" to neighbors for helping to plant seeds or plow the hardened spring soil. One well-known ranching family, the Moultons, celebrated the end of every harvest season by hosting a dance. Community residents two-stepped well into the night by the light of kerosene lanterns as local musicians plucked their fiddles and guitars.

A surprise birthday celebration or wedding of local sweethearts also was time to celebrate. No DJs or event planners were needed for these gatherings. Loud noises from banging pots, bells, and whistles created a festive mood to announce the guests of honor before the dancing and feasting took place.

Think about what it was like getting dressed and ready for one of the big Community Hall dances. Few homes had sinks and running water, so for most people a basin of water was placed on a dresser, in front of a mirror, for washing and shaving. Bathrooms were dark wooden outhouses, so you wouldn't want to spend much time in there! Without hair dryers, nail pol-

ish, or make-up, ladies presented a more natural look and used far less "prep time" than we do today. Men and women wore their best Sunday clothes and made sure their boots and shoes were polished for the special occasion.

Fun was all about spending time together with family and friends. Whether dancing, listening to fiddle music, or sharing the latest news and gossip they had a good time. As guests arrived, they proudly placed their favorite home cooked dishes on tables—savory roasts, crispy fried chicken, lima beans with butter, and black-eyed peas. Homemade frosted layer cakes and berry pies were brought for dessert.

Clara described the site for local happenings like this:

> The Community Hall was the center of social life in the settlement. It was used for socials, 'school exercises,' dinners, bazaars, town meetings, and most and foremost, for country dances, held nearly always on Saturday evenings, when after a long day's work, everybody drove in from the leases and the ranches, young and old, to dance from about eight o'clock to anywhere from midnight to morning. When the children could keep awake no longer, they were wrapped snuggly in blankets and put to bed in the wagons and anterooms.

Besides attending events at the Community Hall, teens back then—as they do today—had get-togethers at their homes. Guys and girls sang and danced to the accompaniment of their guitars and harmonicas while getting to know each other better.

During the week, however, young people had plenty to do in addition to schoolwork. Boys took care of the barn and farm animals, while ironing, washing, and baking were jobs for the girls. Even so, a little extra money could be earned. Once the chores were done, many teenaged boys were allowed to work for neighbors. If a family hired a local boy, this was yet another way a girl could meet an available young man!

In an effort to turn work into fun, the turn-of-the-century *Housewives of Orange County* had their own way of socializing while doing chores. Unlike the wives on the TV show, women gathered to chat and gossip while sewing or "putting up" preserves made from apricots, peaches, and other ripe orchard fruits. Clara was no exception. Her orange marmalade was considered the best around, made from their award-winning Sunkist oranges.

Men took care of the heavy work: plowing, harvesting, and hauling the harvest to the warehouses for railroad shipment. From Clara's writing we know that crops grown in the El Toro area needed to be carefully chosen because water was scarce. For citrus trees to grow, George's brother Frank dug a well on their ranch creating an irrigation system. Water was piped to the trees, especially during the summer months. The hot sun was good, though, for drying their apricot crop on large trays to be shipped to distant markets.

Irrigation improvements took care of water scarcity problems, but another dilemma—wind—could damage the fields and orchards. A solution came in the form of a tree.

Apricots drying on trays

Today, when we talk about the latest crazes, we might think about the newest video game or electronic device. But here is one fad from the days of Old El Toro you may not know about. As the 1890s turned into the 1900s, a kind of tree never before seen in Southern California was all the rage. Hint: It's a favorite of Koala bears.

If you guessed *eucalyptus* you are right! It grows very well in the local soil, since Southern California has a climate similar to the tree's native Australia. More than a hundred years ago, its trunk had many uses. Farmers found the tall, quick-growing trees provided shade for their crops, and when planted in rows, shielded plants from wind. The dense tree trunk burned well as firewood or could be cut into slabs for making furniture. The straight, slender tree trunks made good poles for ship masts and were used on farms for fence posts. Even the sap had a medicinal use as a soothing balm for cuts and wounds. But in time, eucalyptus wood did not prove to be as sturdy as oak or other kinds of lumber. Soon, like almost any game or gadget, the eucalyptus craze was over. All the same, "windrows" of eucalyptus protecting crops from strong Santa Ana winds can still be seen along the borders of Orange County's farms and roadsides.

A windrow of eucalyptus in Irvine, California

With a scarcity of water, dry farming was popular because it involved little irrigation and barley became one of the main dry-farmed crops. In her book, *A History of El Toro*, Clara wrote that "Dry farming is a kind of gambling," meaning a farmer could invest a lot of time and money and not get much back in return.

Clara explained a typical day for a farmhand:

Men were out of the bunkhouse by four o'clock in the morning, each tending and harnessing his own six horses or mules. Breakfast came then, and the men were out in the fields, their stock hitched to the plow by the time it was light enough to see the furrow. At noon the horses were taken from the plow, watered at the water wagon drawn to a convenient spot, and usually fed grain, occasionally hay. A wagon from camp brought the hot dinner. Table and benches were unloaded, shade rigged from the wagon with canvas, and the men sat at ease to eat. Plowing resumed, to continue to late dusk. Unhitched from the plows, each man took his team to camp, unharnessing, feeding, and currying them before going to supper.

Late August was a busy time when the crops were ready to be harvested. Threshing machines separated the grain from the stalks. About 16 men worked the machinery. Other workers stacked bags of grain, cooked meals for the laborers, kept the machinery oiled, and loaded as well as unloaded the wagons. One farmer driving 10 mules could bring in 900 sacks of grain. The drivers (called "mule skinners") brought the grain to a storage warehouse before it was shipped to cities in outlying areas. Often 30 wagons could be seen in a long line, waiting to carry in and deliver the grain. The end of the harvest was a time for the farmers to reward themselves for their hard work, providing yet another reason to celebrate at the Community Hall.

El Toro's Triple A General Store and a horse drawn-wagon filled with bags of grain (Courtesy of First American Title Corporation)

While the men were working together during harvests, club meetings provided a social gathering time for the ranchers' wives. The El Toro Women's Club helped the community by sponsoring social events such as Easter egg hunts for the children, parties, and dinners for visiting agriculturists who studied crop and soil conditions in the area. The ladies also assisted families who were struggling through hard times by providing food, clothing, and other basic necessities to make their lives easier.

Clara soon became a very prominent member of the El Toro Women's Club. Participation in community activities was, in fact, a priority for her. So she was pleased when, in 1938, the club asked her to write *A History of El Toro.* As the first complete written history of the town, it had—and continues to have—great significance. Thanks to Clara's extensive research, we can learn about the area's geographical past, its Native American heritage, the ranchero period, and the earliest days of the community. From her personal remembrances we have an idea of what life was like in the early twentieth century.

Some topics and people were left out of her book. Interestingly, being a soft-spoken and humble woman, Clara wrote very little about herself or her own prominent pioneer family. One especially notorious murder that took place at the El Toro Community Hall was not mentioned at all.

What happened was this: In 1917 someone was shot to death due to mistaken identity.

A man named Horace Munger chose to dance with a young lady. Later that night, outside the hall, her jealous boyfriend, who had eyed them dancing together, aimed and fired a gun at the man he *thought* was Horace. Instead, he had shot and killed an innocent man wearing a sweater similar to the one Horace was wearing. Sadly, the deceased man had been married only a few months earlier, and his wife was expecting their first child. The murderer ran from the law and died before he was ever prosecuted. Did Clara think this story might have marred the good reputation of her hometown, giving people the impression that El Toro was a dangerous place? Or did she decide not to bring up the issue, knowing that it was still a sensitive subject for many El Toro residents at the time? We'll never know for sure why she left out this story in her book.

What is easy to sense from Clara's book about El Toro is that there were aspects about country life in the early days that she yearned for, as life became more complex and modernized. Clara saw the transitions taking place in towns across the nation. She perceived one invention in particular, the automobile, as the cause for so many changes. This new and faster method of transportation would transform small farming communities into crowded towns and even cities. So, it was important to Clara that she write about the uncomplicated life of the early farming community to give future generations a clearer understanding of El Toro's history. She included her opinions about a transformation brought about by new methods of transportation.

Although Clara appreciated how the railroads had transported settlers—such as her family—to remote rural regions, she thought the automobile "wrecked the towns." Goods transported by trucks from warehouses over long distances meant that fewer local men were employed and fewer railroad workers were needed for rail transport. Others, such as telegraph operators, also were no longer being employed by the railroads.

> *Real country life is practically a thing of the past. Every family has an automobile, or two or three, and go 'to town' almost daily, so that the barber shop or lunch counter look in vain for customers, and the grocer no longer serves ranches hiring numbers of men, which in terms of horse travel, were far from other towns.*

Clara viewed modernization as having a negative impact on relationships as well. Before the automobile, neighbors needed to depend on each other, developing stronger community ties. But now cars could transport people easily over great distances, so reliance on neighbors became less important. Clara even felt that the automobile had an impact on dating! A boy used to court and marry the girl next door, she wrote, but "now the 'girlfriend' probably lives miles away, and the boy jumps into his car, and they go to a movie or a dance at the beach."

Her dismay about these changes, however, didn't mean Clara rebelled against *all* modern conveniences. Soon after moving to El Toro, she became the proud owner of a new invention: the washing machine. This innovative device consisted of a wooden tub with a hand-operated plunger. There were, however, no clothes dryers. Instead, clothes were hung on a clothesline to dry in the fresh air. And like everyone else, Clara and George eventually traded in their horse and buggy for an automobile. Reluctantly, they knew they must change with the times, much like many older people today have learned how to use computers and other electronics.

Fortunately, Clara realized she could preserve the simplicity and charm of small town life, as well as the natural beauty of the mountains and beaches, through her art and writing. First, she sketched the landscapes and seascapes, later using them as guides to create her paintings. Recalling her trip to Yosemite National Park with George, where they had traveled by horse and buggy past El Capitan and Bridalveil Falls, Clara was inspired to write poetry describing the breathtaking scenery.

I heard the mighty trumpets of the waterfalls:
And the solemn music of many harps were
The great winds in the lofty pines and the goodly cedars.

Yosemite Valley's Bridalveil Falls
(Courtesy of Barbara Price)

She further created a vivid comparison of the waterfall to the clarity of glass and sheerness of fine netting.

They were carved as of glass;
They were spread with veils.

On their six-month journey, Clara had time to reflect and interpret through her words and imagination, these visual impressions of majestic Yosemite National Park. The couple enjoyed their time together wherever they settled or traveled.

Chapter Eight

REMEMBRANCES

In 1931 George's brother Frank and his family decided to settle in El Toro to live closer to their relatives. Frank and his wife Florence had a nine-year-old daughter named Gwendoline. Gwen is one of the last living relatives who remembers Clara and George. Of course, I wanted to meet Gwen to hear stories about her Aunt Clara and Uncle George. In 2011, my husband and I made a trip to visit Gwen and her husband Boyd in their hometown of Loveland, Colorado.

Gwen remembered the times when her Uncle George took her to the El Toro General Store. He would buy her favorite treats—pieces of sticky-sweet, candy orange slices and as many pitted ripe olives she could eat. Aunt Clara didn't want between-meal snacking to spoil Gwen's appetite before dinner. Without finding any telltale olive pits, she couldn't know how many Gwen had eaten! Uncle George and Gwen would have a good laugh about that.

Clara and George

Among the gifts she received from Uncle George and Aunt Clara was her first Bible. It was personalized with "Gwendoline" engraved in gold on the cover. To this day, she has kept that King James Version of the Bible as a cherished remembrance of her aunt and uncle.

Gwen as well as former residents of El Toro remembered Clara and George as kind and good-hearted neighbors who went out of their way to help others. Some recall holiday seasons when generous-sized cartons filled with fruit, homemade preserves, fresh vegetables, and fried chicken were graciously given from the Fox household.

Clara and George watched Southern California change with each passing decade. In 1929 our country was going through an economic crisis, the Great Depression. Millions were out of work. In response, the government created jobs, such as building roads and bridges. In this way improvements were made in towns and cities while jobs were provided for the unemployed. Farmers and ranchers, including those in El Toro, were hit hard as crop prices dropped. Clara, George, and their neighbors helped each other through the difficult times providing food, jobs, and moral support.

On December 7, 1941 an attack was made on Pearl Harbor, Oahu prompting the United States to enter World War II. That meant workers were needed to build planes, weapons, and other equipment for our military. Women became a larger part of the work force as men went off to war. A training station for the Marines was built near El Toro, employing many local workers.

When the war ended victoriously in 1945, soldiers returned home to marry and start families. A number of servicemen who had been stationed at the El Toro Marine Corps Air Station decided to settle in the area. El Toro remained a farming community at the time, so new homeowners resided in nearby communities such as Santa Ana, Costa Mesa, Tustin, and Buena Park.

Along with a growing population and greater demand for goods and services, further transformation in towns and cities began to take place. Dry goods stores slowly disappeared as large department stores like May Company and Bullock's (known today as Macy's) sold clothing, furniture, and household items. Fewer people patronized the old-fashioned general stores to purchase food items from their limited variety of local farm products. A new kind of store, the "supermarket," carried larger choices of meats, fruits, and vegetables, often shipped in from around the country. A web of highways was connecting cities across the nation.

While much of Orange County was growing and expanding, Laguna Beach remained a quiet beach community in Orange County. When the upkeep of their El Toro property became too much for them, Clara and George moved to Laguna Beach. A short time afterwards they relocated to the inland town of Tustin where George passed away in 1951 at the age of 77.

He received full military honors for his service in the Spanish-American War. Remaining soldiers from his Infantry unit stood at attention by his grave, dressed in military uniforms to pay final respects to their old comrade. As George's casket was slowly lowered into the ground at his family gravesite in Santa Ana, a former soldier solemnly played the traditional "Taps" on his trumpet. No doubt, Clara must have been thankful she answered "Yes" to George's marriage proposal 46 years earlier, as she said her final good bye to the man she loved.

Clara eventually moved back to Laguna Beach to live near her niece, Marge and her family. Her final years were spent living just a few blocks from the beach where she had vacationed and loved to sketch 50 years earlier.

Clara's sketchpad

Here is Clara's interpretation of the sea in Laguna:

> *Wind and ocean*
> *Are mingling in wild commotion.*
> *The waters crash upon the rocky wall,*
> *With thundering roar the breakers fall:*
> *They brawl in forward rushing motion*
>
> *Amethyst, emerald, deep sapphire,*
> *And chips of diamond, sparkling fire,*
> *To sprinkle o'er; the milky play*
> *Of opal here these shallows display.*

Can you picture the sunlight glittering on the ocean like diamonds and hear the low rumble of waves as they repeatedly hit the rocks?

Present day El Toro Road near Raymond Street with Saddleback Mountain in the distance
Lake Forest, California

As predicted by the woman who wrote the history of El Toro, the once rural community has gone through changes, including its name. Lake Forest, as it is known today, is a city with modern shopping centers, rows of tract homes, and wide, well-lit streets.

Grave marker of Clara Mason Fox at the
Santa Ana Cemetery in Santa Ana, California

When Clara was young she traveled along dusty country roads on horseback. By the end of her life in 1959, she had witnessed the dawn of the Space Age with exploration into outer space in rockets. How much the world had changed during Clara's lifetime!

Clara Mason Fox passed away on March 11, 1959 at the age of 85, leaving behind her pencil drawings, oil paintings, family photographs, and writings. She is buried next to her devoted husband George at the

Santa Ana Cemetery in Santa Ana, California. Packed away in Grandma Marge's attic, her possessions were forgotten for many years, until being discovered by a new generation.

I feel lucky to have become the caretaker of the dusty old carton in Marge's attic. Clara reached out to me through her drawings from a century ago and in the faded tracings of handwritten words on paper. Three generations later, the teacher and artist who was Clara, spoke to the teacher and artist I have chosen to become. I like to think that Clara would have been pleased to know that Marge's grandson Jon—himself an artist—would marry someone who appreciated her many accomplishments and who would tell her story to others.

As the idea for this book became clearer, I felt Clara beside me. While I was researching this book in fact, I found myself consulting some of the very same sources (such as books from the Orange County Archives and Santa Ana's Bowers Museum) that Clara had used to write her 1930s book on El Toro. It was as if she was pointing me in the right direction and saying, "If you want to learn more about me, look here." She also, of course, revealed herself to me through her art, photos, and letters found in that box in the attic. Through Clara, I had the privilege of meeting historians, archivists, and even some of Clara's relatives I never knew, such as her niece Gwen Johnson.

As I continued my research for this book, Clara taught me something. Regarding her thoughts on the book, *A History of El Toro*, she wrote:

> *I have been astonished to find how recollections, carefully and honestly recalled, can differ. Every reader will say of some part of this history, 'She has that wrong! It was thus and so!' It may have been, at that, but I have taken a consensus of recalled facts, to find the true one, and have taken pains to make verifications, when memories conflicted.*

When people read a history book, they may have their own interpretation of what was written or believe a statement isn't quite correct. I have learned that authors try to be true to the story and add interest as well. It was as if Clara was providing me direction on how to tell her story through her own words and pictures, and what others had said about her.

Most importantly, I hope I have helped bring to life the story of our own California pioneer heroine. May Clara's story, which began in a time very long ago, be an inspiration to the readers of this book today. Even if we can't all design a Laguna Beach house or write a history book, perhaps Clara's example will help you find your own strengths to express the things that matter to you. We can learn from Clara example how to take problems and challenges in our own lives and use them to help us become stronger and more resilient individuals.

So every once in a while, when you think about how tired you are of homework, chores, or jobs, think of Clara carrying the family's water from a stream to their house in Silverado Canyon. Or how she worked while attending school thousands of miles from home. Also remember to take time, as Clara did, to sketch a scene of something you love or write about the things that are important to *you*.

The Life of Clara Mason Fox
and World Events

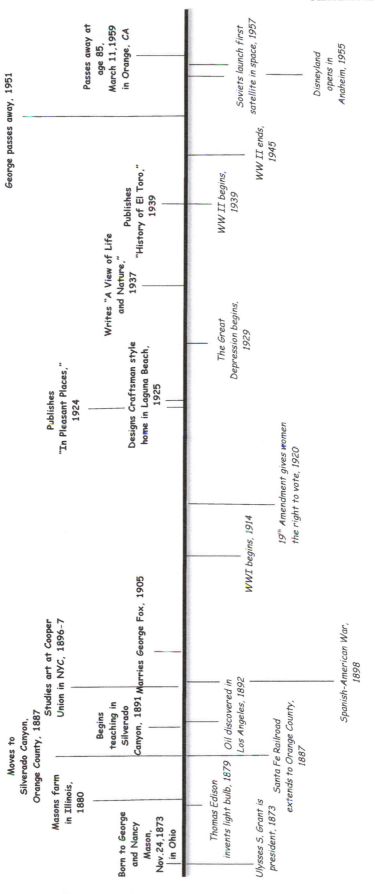

Born to George and Nancy Mason, Nov. 24, 1873 in Ohio

Masons farm in Illinois, 1880

Moves to Silverado Canyon, Orange County, 1887

Begins teaching in Silverado Canyon, 1891

Studies art at Cooper Union in NYC, 1896-7

Marries George Fox, 1905

Publishes "In Pleasant Places," 1924

Designs Craftsman style home in Laguna Beach, 1925

Writes "A View of Life and Nature," 1937

Publishes "History of El Toro," 1939

George passes away, 1951

Passes away at age 85, March 11, 1959 in Orange, CA

Thomas Edison invents light bulb, 1879

Ulysses S. Grant is president, 1873

Oil discovered in Los Angeles, 1892

Santa Fe Railroad extends to Orange County, 1887

Spanish-American War, 1898

WWI begins, 1914

19th Amendment gives women the right to vote, 1920

The Great Depression begins, 1929

WW II begins, 1939

WW II ends, 1945

Disneyland opens in Anaheim, 1955

Soviets launch first satellite in space, 1957

Poems from *In Pleasant Places*
by Clara Mason Fox

DUSK IN THE CANYON

Dusk, deepening in the canyon; dimmer
The trail; the last faint glimmer
Of twilight fading from the upper hill;
A mystic spell my heart enthralling
I take the dim path, to the calling,
The eerie summons of the whipporwill.

A CONTRAST

The sunlight glitters coldly on the snow
That robes the mountain slopes and weights the
pine
Whose rich greens show the darker. Crystal-
line
The chill air hangs, and still. But see! Below,
A sun-steeped valley glimmers in a show
Of color,—a wide mosaic whose design
Is laid in squares of green, with interline
Of white,—the thread-_like roads that come and
go.
Among the orange-groves and grain-fields wind
The streams, like silver ribbons, to the sea
Whose level blue at the horizon lies,
Dimmed in blue haze. A contrast sharp-
defined!
Here,—winter and the calendar agree,
And there,—dwells summer as of Paradise!
February—

ARCH BEACH

Bright golden headlands stepping in the sea,
Fretted by age-long strife of wind and wave
In spanning arch and glooming, yawning cave,
Where still the green waves battle furiously;
Far sea and sky one blue profundity,
And outer sapphire, inner emerald pave
The ocean floor; the breakers, thundering, lave
Each curving beach in foaming bravery,—
A fringe of white to mark the sea's purlieu.
I can but trust that in another plane
Of being, we shall have sensations new
And keener,
Know a fuller life of bliss,
But I've no guess of what I could attain
Of greater joy or beauty than just this.
August—

A CHRISTMAS VISION

Christmas! Magic word that doth restore
Vision of fields enswathed in spotless snow,
Gaunt, bare trees groaning when the keen
winds blow;
Gay groups that gather where the huge fires roar,
With nuts and apples from the cellared store;
A gift-tree glittering in the fire-light glow;—
Thus vision. To my waking eyes doth show
A sunlit scene framed by my open door,
Green trees and velvet grass, a balmy air
Luring me forth to Christmas trees low-bowed
With weight of golden fruit or roses fair,—
Rare gifts to bless the lowly, shame the proud.
Ah, sweetly here the angels once again
Cry clearly, Peace on earth, good-will to men!
December—

THE LAGUNA PAINTERS

A range of hills here marks the changing shore
Of a deep sea whose lucent waters run
In splendid colors to its cliffs of dun
And tawny gold. Here lies the watery floor
In glorious greens, and purples, blue at fore
To distant indigo. Each turn is won
A picture new and each more perfect seeming.
The jutting headlands, golden-beaming,
Are planted in the sea, whose green tide lift
And throw themselves in spray white-gleaming
Upon the rocky slopes, and, backward stream-
ing,
Pour whitening to the coming waves, the drift
Of seaweed left in wreaths in every rift
Or cleft of rock, where wind and wave
Have fretted gargoyles, cornice, peristyles;
And they have cut off little golden isles
And black and rugged rocks, all honeycombed
and eaten;
Or long, low hedges that still forward creep
Onto the deeper sea, where o'er them sweep
The heaving swells, that, mangled, foaming,
beaten,
A whitened smother show upon the emerald
deep.
Between the points lie little crescent beaches,
Curves of palely-gleaming sand,
And o'er the opalescent shallower reaches
The swells come surging strongly toward the
land,
They tower, and greenly break, and on the
strand
They fling their lacy scallops.
Wind and ocean
Are mingling in wild commotion.
The waters crash upon the rocky wall,

With thundering roar the breakers fall;
They brawl in forward rushing motion,
To sink away into a heaving sigh;
Then o'er they sand they whisper, lisp,
Returning wavelets curling crisp
Above the rippling sands they lave.
The little wading sea-birds cry,
So plaintive-sweet, and, sweeping by
The wind goes roaring through his rocky caves.
But not one sound we hear alone,
For all are mingled with the deep, sad tone,
The voice of the unresting waves,-
Are merged into a monotone
Of grief. But yet, the sadness and the sound
Are but the hem upon the outer bound
Of that vast drapery
Of calm and silence, deep, profound,
That wraps the sleeping sea;
The restless movement but the bright embroid-
ery
Wrought by the winds on the eternal peace that
broods
Upon the watery solitudes.

And when you pass, on either hand
The busy painters you will see;
Upon the cliffs, upon the sand,
Their wide-umbrellaed easels stand,
And there they work engrossedly.
Upon the sea with gaze intent,
Then from the range of rainbow hues
Some bits of color they will choose,
To be upon their palettes blent.

With head drawn back, and eyes half-closed,
The strokes of color are disposed
Upon the waiting canvas;—then

Upon the sea they gaze again.
O busy painters, what can ye do?
If your gods be kind, and ye be true,
With your pastes of ore, and your bits of clay
The rounded hills ye might build anew,
With yellow ochre these cliffs portray;
Your madder, gamboge, indigo
Again be made to live and grow
In gray-green brush on their fair plateau.
But what of the wonder of the sea?
Can mauve or cobalt blue, or green,
Can iron, copper, zinc, or lead
Dead chrome or sodium, ultramarine,
Depict this lucid ocean bed?
A palette of gems ye would require
This limpid floor would ye inlay,—
Amethyst, emerald, deep sapphire,
And chips of diamond, sparkling fire,
To sprinkle o'er; the milky play
Of opal here these shallows display.

And when your coloring is done,
The real painting ye have but begun.
For God has worked this fair design
With more than color, more than line,
For He has painted, too, with wind and sun
The light, the glow, the salty air,
Sea-flavored; yea, and He has painted there
With ceaseless movement and unending sound;
Has wrought relief of glittering strife upon a
ground
Of still blue peace.
Can ye ensnare
In paint the movement on the beaches?
Can ye add the thunder, or the moan and sigh,
The salty-tang, the sea-bird's cry?
Can ye paint the lure of the indigo reaches,

That, when the eye would rest, beseeches,
And draws it on and on unendingly?
From what dull tube can ye express
The peace that lies upon this sea?
Can ye show rest in strife, in power, tender-
ness?
Or paint this thought of God and of eternity?
Yea, He has set a model there
To drive a struggling painter to despair;
To lure him on with stretches vast,
With thousand pictures, color fair,
And then to humble him at last.
But he may think he has done much
If in his study he shall bring
Away with him the faintest touch
Of beauty thus divine, of this rare coloring,
Some hint of feeling to his canvas cling.
And surely, sitting there, alone,
In stillness, working patiently,
There shall be something in the waves' deep
tone
Will speak to him; some of the beauty of the
sea
Pass in his soul; some of its peace become his
own,
Some of its power, its sublimity.

AT SUNSET

Against the fiery west each sharp-limned tree
To specter shape of charcoal black has burned:
'Twixt flaming sky and redly molten sea
The distant isle to gray-blue ash has urned.
Ah, dear, dead day! How, fit thy funeral pyre
With leagues of sea and sky one blazing fire.

A Final Note

Something unexpected happened while I was writing this book. I received an email from a friend, journalist Janet Whitcomb, saying she had come across a press release published by The Rancho Santa Ana Botanic Garden (RSABG) about Clara Mason Fox. In 2010 RSABG personnel had discovered a number of exquisite watercolors depicting a variety of wildflowers found in Orange County. With the earliest ones dated 1894, they had apparently been forgotten for 50 years or more in the research library's cabinet drawers. The paintings were filed with collections of dried plant samples. The artist was Clara Mason Fox.

Comparing Clara's earlier pencil sketches to her vibrant watercolor paintings are like looking at a black-and-white photo compared to a HD video. The pastel and jewel-tone colors look amazingly bright and fresh, as though they had been recently painted. The detailed flowers and leaves have a three-dimensional quality. Some illustrations include hand written scientific explanations. Others look like works in progress showing light pencil outlines. To date, more than 150 have been found and more are expected to be uncovered as the cataloging continues.

In 2010 Jessica Dewberry, an intern from the Getty Foundation, was assigned to research the paintings for accuracy and digitize the images. She became intrigued with the artist who had created the mini-masterpieces. She wondered, Who was Clara Mason Fox? Jessica searched for biographical information but could find only references to Clara's birth, death, and that she had been inspired by the beauty of Silverado Canyon. My husband and I met with Jessica and other researchers at the RSAGB library to provide the details we knew about Clara's life. They were amazed to hear about Clara's achievements as a teacher, poet, and author.

We were pleased to learn that the watercolors were deemed to be of such artistic importance that the Huntington Library in San Marino, California decided to show the paintings along with other well-known botanical painters in an exhibit called "When They Were Wild: Recapturing California's Wildflower Heritage."

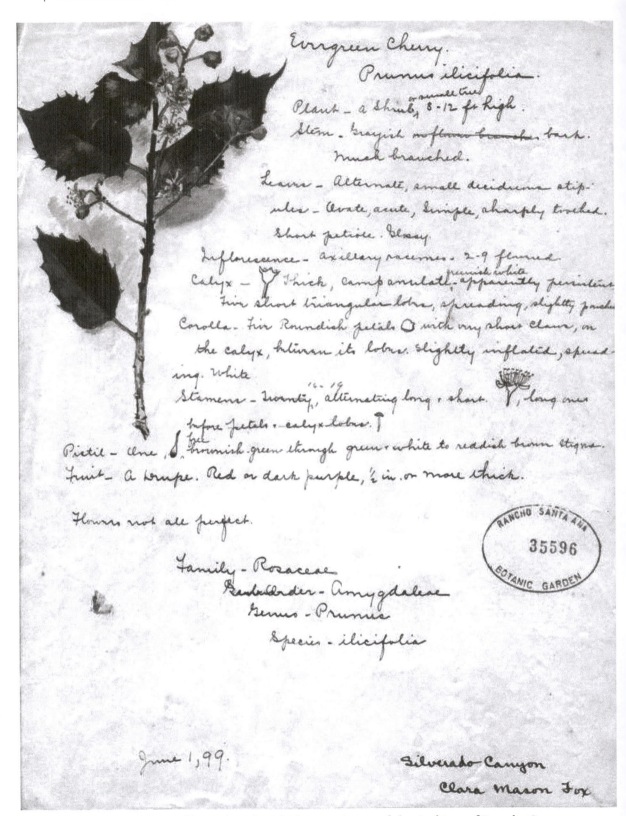

Evergreen Cherry (Reproduced with the permission of the Archives of Rancho Santa Ana Botanic Garden, Claremont, CA)

One of the most recent discoveries has been a seascape painting found in a closet where it was stored for 25 years. Coated with several layers of varnish and grime, the oil painting was carefully restored to its original radiance. The calm phosphorescent waters of Laguna Beach stretch toward the seashell-pink horizon in this small-sized oil painting with Clara's signature written in pencil.

Rescued from obscurity, Clara's life and accomplishments are being rediscovered and illuminated for all to recognize and appreciate. As she continues to reveal herself through her art and writings, I wonder what future discoveries about Clara Mason Fox might be found.

Laguna Seascape

Resources

"American History Timeline 1780-2005." www.Animatedatlas.com.

"American Memory." Library of Congress, http://www.loc.gov.

"Blizzard of 1888." http://www.vny.cuny.edu/blizzard.

California Census Records. 1900, 1910, 1920, 1930. National Archives.

Cooper Union Annual Reports, May 29, 1896 and May 29, 1897.

Cooper Union Women's Art School Book of Rules and Regulations. ca. 1885-87.

"Craftsman Bungalow House Style." http://architecture.about.com.

"Discovery of Oil in Los Angeles." http//www.usc.edu/libraries/archives/la/oil.html.

" Disneyland's History." http://www.justdisney.com/disneyland/history.html.

Fox, Clara Mason. *A History of El Toro*. Lake Forest, California: El Toro Woman's Club, 1938.

Fox, Clara Mason. *A View of Life and Nature: Poems*. El Toro, California: Unpublished Mimeographed Document, 1937-1938.

Fox, Clara Mason. *In Pleasant Places*. Los Angeles, California, Grafton Publishing Corporation, 1924.

"Frontier Trails of the Old West." http://www.frontiertrails.com/butterfield htm.

"The Homestead Act." http://www.nps.gov/archive/home/homestead_act.html.

Illinois Census Records. 1880. National Archives.

Johnson, Gwendoline and Boyd. *The John Syndol Fox and Margaret Elizabeth Spear Story.* Loveland, Colorado: Unpublished Document, 2005.

"Lamplighters of Olde Middle Village." www.junipercivic.com/.

"Lincoln's Cooper Union Address Propelled Him to the White House." Robert McNamara, http://About.com.

McClelland, Elsie. *Silverado Canyon Sketches:* 1853-1953. Historical Society of Southern California, 1957.

Miller, Ilana, "The Victorian Era." http://victoriaspast.com.

Naylor, Natalie N. (editor). *Journeys on Old Long Island.* Interlaken, New York: Empire State Books, 2002.

"Orange County Great Park." http://www.ocgp.org/learn/history.

Orange County Historical Commission. *A Hundred Years of Yesterdays.* Orange County, California: Orange County Historical Commission, 2004.

Osterman, Joe. *The Old El Toro Reader: A Guide to the Past.* Whittier, California: Old El Toro Press, 1992.

_____. *Stories of Saddleback Valley.* Whittier, California: Old El Toro Press, 1992.

Payne, Theodore. *Theodore Payne in His Own Words.* Pasadena, California: Many Moon Press, 2004.

Pleasants, J.E. *History of Orange County.* Los Angeles, California: J.R. Fennell and Sons, 1931.

Ramsey, Merle and Mabel. *Pioneer Days of Laguna Beach.* Laguna Beach, California, Mission Printing Company, 1967.

Silverado Files. BX3/30, Silverado Public Library. Silverado, California.

Valentino, Thomas. "Farming in Young Illinois." www.lib.niu.edu/2000.

"Women's History in America." http://www.wic.org.

"World Events." http:// www.infoplease.com.

"Yosemite." www.nps.com.

Interviews

Barrios, Russ. Pitcher Park Docent, Beekeeping in Orange County, Orange, CA, September 9, 2011.

Johnson, Gwendoline and Boyd, George and Clara Fox's niece and husband, Loveland, CO. August 1, 2009, August 9, 2011.

Whitcomb, Janet. Modjeska House and Gardens Docent, County of Orange Historical Parks, February 11, 2012.

CPSIA information can be obtained at www.ICGtesting.com
Printed in the USA
BVOW101959180313

315847BV00003B/7/P